ESSAYS ON RELIGION

ESSAYS ON RELIGION

ARTHUR CLUTTON-BROCK

WITH AN INTRODUCTION BY

CANON B. H. STREETER, F.B.A.

ESSAY INDEX

Essay Index Reprint Series

BOOKS FOR LIBRARIES PRESS

FREEPORT, NEW YORK

First Published 1926
Reprinted 1969

STANDARD BOOK NUMBER:
8369-1078-8

LIBRARY OF CONGRESS CATALOG CARD NUMBER:
79-84302

PRINTED IN THE UNITED STATES OF AMERICA

CONTENTS

INTRODUCTION

I N form, this book is a collection of Essays any one of which may be read by itself. In fact, they represent a continuous effort, during three years of intermittent illness, of a man haunted by the feeling that the religion by which he had been living had been too cheaply won, to find some solution, more profound than hitherto, of the problem posed by the discord between man's highest values and the facts of the universe revealed by science. And they were written as a series of preliminary studies for what at times he hoped might prove to be his most serious contribution to human thought.

Arthur Clutton-Brock during the latter part of his life exercised a wide influence, but one of an uniquely individual kind, on religious thinking in English-speaking countries—more especially among the younger generation. But it was not until he had reached the age of forty-eight that he displayed any special concern with Religion, and, when he did so, his approach to it was identical with his approach to Literature and Art. Accordingly, an attempt to trace the development of his mind and activities in this particular sphere would seem to be worth making for its intrinsic interest. It is, moreover, almost necessary for the understanding of the trend and significance of the last phase of his mental evolution which finds expression in the present volume. So far as possible, I shall do this in his own words; for, to an extent that is rare with writers on religion, it can be said of Clutton-Brock that "the style is the man." The peculiar individuality of his contribution to religion cannot be appreciated apart from the way in which it is expressed.

Christ, Shakespeare and Mozart are the names which recur most frequently in his later writings; and the love and admiration that he had for all three were in the first place elicited by the outstanding beauty of that to which they gave expression. To him all great art was inspired; and all real religion was inspiration.

The man who is filled with the Grace of God has opened his mind, not only to all the beauty of the earth and sky, but to all things in action and thought that are of the same nature as beauty. Passively he has experienced them as if his mind were a meadow steeped in moonlight; and actively he gives them out again, having made them his own with all his own character in them.

Christ is the supreme Master of the art of life, whose words are music and whose life

Introduction

a poem, just because of that precision and
completeness of meaning which gives them the
quality of a perfect work of art.

We can imagine a worldly man listening to Christ
as the master of a strange new art worth learning.
And it seems so easy ; he does not strive or cry over
it ; he is not a professor. He is himself a man of the
world and something more, the man of another world,
one who has not even refused the kingdom of this
world but has transcended it, turning from jewels to
flowers like a child.

The chapter on Christ in *Studies in Christianity* is written in a spirit not essentially different
from that in which he wrote the article for
Shakespeare's tercentenary in the *Literary
Supplement* of *The Times* ; and for that reason
it is probably a treatment of the theme unique
in English literature.

Christ is the greatest figure in history as Hamlet is
the greatest figure in art, because of his reality ; and
he still has the power because of this reality to make
men fall in love with him in spite of all their prejudices.

A Christian is

one who has fallen in love with Christ ; and the peculi-
arity of the Christian religion and of the Christian
character springs out of this fact. . . . When we love a
great artist and are utterly subdued to his art, it is
not because of his powers, which we do not possess,
but because of the self, which is also ourselves, that
he reveals to us. The powers only reveal ; and the
more they reveal the more simple and human they
seem, so that his supreme triumph over us is to make
us feel that we could do it all ourselves, that we are,

with him, doing it all ourselves. And so it is with
Christ. We feel that we could ourselves accomplish
not the miracles, which are to us, as they were to him,
nothing, but the life, the character. He does not
make his state of being hard to us but easy, not
mysterious but simple. You can do it yourselves, if
you will, he says—The Kingdom of Heaven is within
you.

It is by the best in ourselves, in Christ, that we
know God. If there is a God, we are the sons of God ;
and Christ is one of us. He has his authority for us
because he is utterly one of us and not because he is
in any way different ; and the more he is himself to
us, the less authority or status he needs, whether
human or divine. I do not need to think that The
Magic Flute is more than human, before I can be aware
of its beauty. If it were not beautiful to me, if it
were not wise as only such beauty can be, what value
to me would it have, even if I knew that it had been
communicated straight from God ? In The Magic
Flute, in Christ, in all men and things that make us
aware of divinity, the Word is utterly made flesh.
And we cannot make it more the Word by thinking
that there is in the flesh some difference from our own.

Clutton-Brock's early enthusiasm, after
Shakespeare, was first for Shelley and later on
for William Morris, on both of whom he wrote
books of penetrating insight. And his own
development was akin to that of William
Morris in that his approach to life came
naturally in the first place through the sense
of beauty, and it was out of and through his
æsthetic passion that his interest in social and
religious questions grew. His delight in music
was passionate in its quality. He once told

Introduction

me that this had come to him quite suddenly
when he was about the age of twenty in an
experience which he likened to religious con-
version. But his interest in religion, which
was born much later, came in no such cata-
clysmic way: it was a slow and gradual
development.

The series of articles in *The Times Literary
Supplement* in the autumn of 1914 (afterwards
reprinted as *Thoughts on the War*) were in no
way concerned with religious topics in the
technical sense of that term, but they displayed
a quality of ethical insight which marked him
out as a man with an essentially religious
message. Shortly after the appearance of
these articles he began to get invitations—the
earliest, I think, came from the Student
Christian Movement—pressing him to give
occasional lectures on topics of a semi-religious
character.

In June 1916 came his book, *The Ultimate
Belief.*

When I began this little book (he writes), I meant it
for teachers. My object was to state very simply
certain beliefs about the nature of man and of the
universe, which, as it seems to me, children ought to
be taught, so that their minds may be protected
against sophistries old and new. But, as I wrote, I
found that I was trying to make these beliefs more
clear to myself.

Essays on Religion

The words are no conventional apology. Everything that he wrote about religion was the expression of an effort to reach out after something to which he felt he had not yet quite attained, or to make clear to himself something which he had only just attained. That is why everything he has to say on this over-written subject is always fresh and real. He is never repeating things which have come to him from the tradition of the elders ; he is always seeking, and often captures, a new impression.

The Ultimate Belief is not the theological treatise which the title might suggest. It is rather an attempt to limn out a philosophy of education, and therefore of life, based on the eliciting of that spontaneous delight—which he believed to be innate in humanity, when unspoilt by false schooling—in the triad of what he used to call the " absolute values," Goodness, Beauty and Truth.

We are apt to think of love as if it were a merely moral feeling ; but love is the realization of the absolute value of things outside us, which is attained to intellectually and æsthetically no less than morally. While we value things outside us in terms of our own well-being, we cannot love at all. For self-love is only a metaphor. Love is good, but self-love is bad ; therefore it is not love. What we call self-love is merely a failure to love, a failure to see absolute value in what is outside ourselves. But when I love beauty or truth, I escape from self-love no less than

Introduction

when I love goodness. . . . There is in every human being the passionate desire for this self-forgetfulness, and a passionate delight in it when it comes. The child feels that delight among spring flowers ; we can all remember how we felt it in the first apprehension of some new beauty of the universe, when we ceased to be little animals, and became aware that there was this beauty outside us to be loved. And most of us must remember, too, the strange indifference of our elders. They were not considering the lilies of the field ; they did not want us to get our feet wet among them.

In 1916–17 he wrote a number of the articles on religion which have become a regular feature of the Saturday issue of *The Times*. Though unsigned, his work could always be identified by the individuality of his literary style. It is hoped that a selection from these will be reprinted at some future date.

My own acquaintance with Clutton-Brock began early in 1915 ; and from the end of that year till his last illness he was one of the most regular attendants at the groups which met at Cumnor for the discussion of philosophic, social and religious problems at the house of the late Miss Lily Dougall. He contributed two essays to each of two Symposia, *Immortality* (1917) and *The Spirit* (1919), produced by these groups and edited by myself. Into these essays, he averred, he put more time and thought than into any other of his

xiii

definitely religious writings. In them we notice especially the peculiar quality of his repulsion to everything mechanical—whether in the form of a materialistic conception of the universe or of the mentality which loves mechanical conventionality in art, conduct or religious tradition—and his peculiar apprehension of the reality of the spiritual, and the way in which he made the conception of absolute values, in beauty, truth and goodness, the one test of the genuinely spiritual.

Either spirit is the supreme fact, supreme over all changes of process and lasting through them all ; or life is to be defined as a mechanical process suffering from the illusion that it is not mechanical. In which case nothing distinguishes it from not-life except the illusion. If that be so, all our values are part of that superfluous illusion which is the essence of life. . . . The mechanical process is capable of knowing that it is one ; a remarkable triumph no doubt, but one which necessarily must tempt it to the doubt whether it is a mechanical process after all. . . . Thus there must always be a reaction against all mechanical theories of life just as inevitable as the reaction against all spurious certainties of supernatural belief.

Speaking of the unconscious causes which predispose so many men of noble character to a disbelief in immortality, he writes :

This refusal to believe in a future life is the supreme example of man's passion for disinterestedness. It is the most resolute and defiant of all possible answers to the question—Doth Job fear God for nought ?

Introduction

The answer is—Yes, even though there be no God, and though he who fears is but a quintessence of dust, for a moment become conscious of itself. That is the last asceticism of which man in his passion for absolute values is capable. He proclaims them in the face of a universe which he asserts to be utterly indifferent to them. But this asceticism is never, I think, the complete disbelief it supposes itself to be. Rather it is a kind of self-denial, a discipline which the mind imposes on itself that it may be sure that its values are absolute.

The mind of man is at the present day suffering from a nervous shock caused by his past failures to conceive of a future state. A burnt child dreads the fire ; and the mind of man has been burnt by the fires of his own imagined Hell. So he flinches from the peril of any more conceiving.

Very characteristic of him is the suggestion that Heaven is life freed from the " irrelevance " of the struggle to go on living ; and that therefore art is a kind of prophecy of Heaven.

All rhythm is a prophecy of a freer state of being, a state in which man escapes from the struggle for life to the expression of his own values, his own ideals ; and in all art, the more completely it is art, there is the sense of heaven, whether it be a triumphant prophecy of it or an aching desire for it. Even in despair the artist conjures up the freedom of that heaven of which he despairs ; for he expresses his despair in the free speech of heaven.

A friend, who had met him for the first time, once remarked to me, " A couple of hours of Clutton-Brock's ' table-talk ' is worth a journey from the Antipodes." In his conversation a predominant feature was the keen humour which was never absent for any long time. But when he wrote on Literature and Art, the expression of humour was rather severely kept in check. It was otherwise in his religious writings. This was only partly due, I think, to reaction from conventional solemnity; it was mainly because to him religion was a thing essentially spontaneous— an expression of the delight in beauty and the zest of living. Thus it came natural to him, when writing on religion, to write with the gay freedom of his conversation among friends—a freedom that shocked some of his admirers, but endeared him to the young.

I imagine to myself Henry James in Heaven. If it were the conventional state of blessedness, what a polite but persistent note of interrogation he would sound in it; how he would still labour incessantly to find the phrase that would exactly describe his dislike of it.

A woman sitting next to you at a concert, fans herself, munches chocolates, and looks at her nose in a bag-mirror; so we are estranged from each other and filled with thoughts of murder. (Then he goes on.) The chief purpose of worship is to draw us into the fellowship of spiritual experience; and it is a useful rule of decorum that people should not fan themselves in church or eat chocolates or look at their noses in a bag-mirror. They know that in church such behaviour would prevent the fellowship of spiritual experience. But unfortunately there is another, more

Introduction

servile motive for decorum in church. We must behave ourselves there lest God should be offended; and so church-goers put up with much in their services that cannot produce any spiritual experience, because they think they acquire merit by being bored. It is as if they were listening to a dull play at Court. One does not criticize the drama as it is performed at Windsor; one acquires merit by being there.

In 1918 he published with Messrs. Constable *Studies in Christianity*, a book which perhaps represents the most buoyantly happy mood in the evolution of his religious thought and feeling. I yield to the temptation of adding to the quotations already made from this work.

We know how Christ would have smiled at anyone who was trying to be Aristotle's ideal man, or the superman, or the German notion of a hero. . . . (These) all behave as if the universe were their washpot; and this behaviour of theirs is supposed to be ideal. So those who follow these ideals can do nothing but behave as if the universe were also their washpot, which it never is. Their conduct is absurd; and it is only a question how long they will be able to keep it up. . . . Every one of us in youth has his dreams of being a great general, a great orator, a great artist, or something else very great. But in these dreams, which we call our ideals, it is never ourselves that are changed, but the universe that consents to be our washpot. Armies go down before us like ninepins; crowds hang on our lips; duchesses weep and fling flowers when we fiddle to them. But we do not know how we annihilate the enemy; we cannot put this eloquence of ours into words; nor can we play the fiddle. It is ourselves, just as we are, with all our

natural incompetence, that triumph; and the ideal is
in the triumph, not in a changed self. . . . The
superman cannot impose his will on the universe; he
can only behave as if he had imposed it, and be
for ever acting the part of a stage king off the
stage.

Freedom is to be found in man's complete surrender
to his values. He must utterly forget himself in them
and forget all the temptations and intimidations of
the world. Compared with them, duty itself is the
world as much as ambition; and, if a man surrenders
himself to his own values, if he hears in them the voice
of God, then he will utterly forget his own status in
every form which it may take. He will not be to himself wise or good, any more than he will be well born;
he will be neither proud nor ashamed of himself. And
therein will be his freedom. . . . The Stoic morality,
even, did not quite free the Stoic of the sense that he
had acquired wisdom; it was based on his pride in
what he had made himself. Marcus Aurelius is always
telling himself that he must bear with mankind because
they are like children. But Christ said, " Suffer
little children to come unto me, and forbid them not :
for of such is the Kingdom of Heaven "—and what is
more, we are sure that he meant it. . . . That is
what Christian humility means; there is nothing
slavish or oriental about it. The Christian is not
humble so that he may please God; he is humble
because he is a child of God and all other men are
children of God too, so what can he have to be proud
of ? He and all men are children of God; they are
not grown up, not middle-aged and accomplished and
dull. The wisdom of the ages is not behind them but
before them; the book of the universe has not all been
read; they are just learning to read snatches of it.
Their father teaches them lessons and they must
listen to them, wondering, never saying, " We have
heard all that before."

Introduction

On one side of his nature there was in Clutton-Brock a certain kinship to the mystics. The *Confessions* of Augustine made a special appeal to him on this side. One of his favourite quotations was: "I asked the heavens, sun, moon and stars; 'nor (say they) are we the God whom thou seekest,' and I replied . . . 'Ye have told me of my God that ye are not He; tell me something of Him,' and they cried all with a great voice, 'He made us.' My questioning them was my mind's desire and their beauty was their answer." But his mysticism, unlike that of the passionate and introspective African, began not from inward conflict but from the vividness of his appreciation of natural beauty. In his essay *Spiritual Experience* in our symposium *The Spirit* this finds striking expression.

Some years ago I was in the Maritime Alps in June, and I came to a spring in the shade of a sweet-chestnut tree on the southern slope of the mountain. Then I knew suddenly how southern peoples had come by their myth of the water-nymph. Standing myself in the blazing sunshine, I almost saw a water-nymph among the waters of the shade. Water-nymphs had always seemed to me frigid, unreal fancies; but now the spring, in its shadowed beauty and contrast with the parched heat of the mountain-side, became alive, became almost a person. It was not the legend of the water-nymph that brought her to my mind: it was the life and beauty of the stream that almost brought her to my eyes. The stream seemed so clearly to be occupied with a lovely, friendly business of its

xix

own that I almost saw a lovely, friendly creature doing it. Then, for a moment, I knew what Paganism meant and why it was believed. I was a pagan myself, and saw what faith and beauty we have lost with it.

But he was always feeling after something richer and deeper than this pagan nature-mysticism, as in the passage that concludes the next essay *Spirit and Matter*. Here keen argument and bantering humour are a half-disguise to something very like the yearning passion of the authentic Christian mystic.

The doctrine of evolution, rightly held, makes us aware that the advance, or the desire for it, is universal. In all things there is life groaning and travailing to become more life, first in mere sensation, then in consciousness ; life hardly differentiated in plants, in animals differentiated, in man personal. And we suffer from our loneliness in the universe because all things that we see have less life than we ourselves ; that is the penalty of our precedence, of our greater consciousness of what life is. We demand more life . . . matter not fully mastered drags us back into the relation of use. The life in us seems insecure, and we see all things as means of securing it. But seeing them so we misunderstand them. . . . God did not make the sun to be our candle. He did not make dogs to be our pets, or midges so that we might learn not to blaspheme when they bite us. He made all things not for us but to Himself, so that they might more and more attain to that life which is Himself. So long as we see the universe in the relation of use to ourselves, it remains cold, indifferent, meaningless to us ; but when we see it in relation to God, sharing the life which is God, but sharing it even more imperfectly than ourselves, then the process of nature is no longer

Introduction

a meaningless, intimidating mechanism, but pathetic
and forgivable to us even as we are to ourselves.
Restless are the hearts of all things until they rest in
Thee.

At the beginning of 1919 he published
What is the Kingdom of Heaven? This was
an attempt to work out at length the idea that
when Christ used this phrase He spoke of a
mystical experience—a vision of a divine
harmony which He apprehended as present
now and here to all those who, like Himself,
had eyes to see it. I feel no doubt that behind
this theory of Clutton-Brock's lay some
mystical experience of his own. But, as so
often happens in the lives of those who enjoy
such experience, the vision of the divine
harmony was followed by the Dark Night of
the Soul. I am not suggesting that in his
case either the Illumination or the Darkness of
the spiritual reaction had the intensity of the
experiences recorded by the great mystics.
But it is significant that at about this time
he more than once remarked to Mrs. Clutton-
Brock that he felt he had attained to his religious
optimism too easily and too cheaply. Moreover, the first part of the fragment printed as
Essay I in this volume bore the date 1920.
It was clearly intended as the opening chapter
of a book, and reflects the mood of a man
struggling with cosmic despair.

Essays on Religion

Henceforward he turned his thoughts with greater intensity, but less of the old light-heartedness, on to the religious quest. The paper on *Home*, printed at the beginning of the posthumous volume *Essays on Life*—with its passionate expression of man's sense of his homelessness in the universe—belongs, I think, to this period.

> Nothing is so beautiful as a light in a cottage window, except the light of the stars; and when we feel the beauty of the cottage light, we know that it is of the same nature as the beauty of the stars—and our desire is to be sure that the stars are the lights of home with the same spirit of home behind them.

His resolute quest was not without reward. It must have been, so far as I can remember, early in 1921 that he spoke to me almost enthusiastically of a new approach to the problem of evil which he was engaged in working out. Essays IV and V, reprinted by the kind permission of the Editor from *The Atlantic Monthly*, and the fragment printed as Essay VI, represent the line of thought on which he had embarked. But when I saw him again some months later, he had put this on one side in order to work out what he thought an even more fruitful line of thought which he described as a new Logic of God. The Essay printed under that title I have been able to piece together from two in-

complete sketches by supplying a few connecting sentences from my recollections of
the line of argument as he then developed it.
But the earlier stages of the internal disease,
which, after three operations, ultimately
proved fatal, prevented the carrying out of his
scheme of working up all this material into
a new philosophy of theism. He was still a
regular member of the staff of *The Times*
newspaper, and he felt bound—especially in
view of the very great consideration accorded
to him by the Management during his long
intervals of severe illness—to give to his
literary work for *The Times* the greater part
of his residual energies.

About a month before his death I stayed
in the house for a few days. He had been for
many weeks confined to his bed, but for four
or five hours each day he talked in his old
style and with his old enthusiasm of every
subject grave and gay in heaven or on earth. In
between attacks of illness he had lately written
the paper *The Religion of the Particular*, printed
as Essay II. The moment I arrived he made
me read the MS., and I could see from the
way in which he asked for my opinion on it,
that he was apprehensive that his mental
power might have failed him before he had
set down something which he felt was of value
to the world. He was enormously cheered and

relieved when I assured him that I thought that it contained some new and important thinking. It was, he explained, intended to carry a stage further the argument of the essay *Spirit and Matter* in our symposium *The Spirit*, which, he then told me, he had always regarded as his most serious contribution to philosophy. Though unfinished, the paper has a certain completeness, and I have printed it, not only because of the importance which he himself attached to it, but also because it does seem, in the context in which it is placed, to fill a gap in the argument. Essay VII is made up of a short piece published in *The Times* and a longer, which might have been written as a sequel, from the *Literary Supplement*. A fine treatment of a great theme, it seemed to me so characteristic of the spirit of the man as to make a worthy conclusion to the book.

The collection of essays here printed is thus a torso, an unfinished attempt to find a new and constructive philosophy of religion. If the reader is prepared to make due allowance for the conditions under which they were written, and for the fact that some of them have had to be pieced together from incomplete fragments, and, disregarding minor inconsistencies or occasional repetitions, will look out for original and living thought, he will

Introduction

find in them much that is new, and much that is, I think, important.

But Arthur Clutton-Brock never quite got back to the happy confidence of his earlier period. Still, at times, he had moments of depression, in which he felt man to be a homeless wanderer, an outcast from the beauty of visible things, and doubted if their beauty was a true answer to his questionings as to the meaning of the universe. On Christmas Day, 1923, just a fortnight before his death, he had dictated to his wife a couple of verses; which have since been printed by Messrs. Benn in the posthumous collection *The Miracle of Love and Other Poems*.

> Now my body masters me
> Little past its pains I see,
> Yet I remember Christmas Day
> Faint and still and far away.
>
> I a man by sickness worn
> On this day when Christ was born,
> Turn for help to that strange story
> All humility mixed with glory.

After a while he asked that the words ' Turn for help ' should be changed to ' Turn again.' " I am not certain that I expect help from it; but I am always thinking of it."

Nevertheless, the religion which had come to him through his love of beauty—and had been honestly served and truthfully expressed

by him as far as he was able in all he did or
wrote—did stay by him to the end, and
upheld him through the long pain and slow
wasting of his body, and enabled him to take
delight in beauty to the very end. A few days
before he died, hearing read the words, " God
said, Let there be light, and there was light,"
he had remarked, " Longinus gives that as
an example of the sublime " ; and on his last
day, after listening intently to the reading of
the passage in the Revelation of St. John
describing the descent of the New Jerusalem,
though he had almost ceased to speak, he
said, " That is the supreme example of the
sublime." His last conscious act was to
point out to his doctor the beauty of an iris ;
and, when he could express it no longer in
word or gesture, this religion gave to his face
a clear-cut beauty of character which, in
its expression of the calm that has transcended
pain, was likened by one standing by to a dead
Christ carved in ivory by a mediæval artist.

March, *1926*   B. H. S.

ESSAYS ON RELIGION

I

The Visionaries⌒   ⌒   ⌒   ⌒

WHENEVER we think deeply or feel deeply about any matter, whenever we give our attention to those works of the past or present in which men have expressed deep feeling or thought, whether they be in words or in sounds alone, or in colour and form, or in things of use such as buildings or even pottery, we are always aware of something implied but not said, something that gives likeness and a peculiar common value in all that diversity to whatever is deeply thought or felt. Without this something implied, the works of man of whatever kind seem to be contrivances of the moment, useful perhaps or amusing, but hand-to-mouth, and like our own routine experience without any settled or lasting value to us. All the books that interest us for the moment, or that have a quaint interest to us out of the past, all the theories that tickle us with their novelty or have as we say a

I

" historic interest," the myths we study so that we may understand the workings of the human mind : these things are to us things of history, if they belong to the past, or matters of amusement or business if to the present. They lack that implication of which we are constantly aware when we ourselves think or feel most deeply and which we recognize in those other works of the past that are not past but present.

What is that implication ? What is the un-said thing which is eternally said deep in our own minds and in all things that remain pre-sent to our minds, though the men who made them may have lived in Asia thousands of years ago ?

Here we, living in England in the twentieth century, are occupied with a thousand things of the moment and often things necessary to our existence. In our world of use and wont we are surrounded with familiar things : cups and saucers, out of which we drink our tea, news-papers which tell us in our own tongue that which we wish to believe ; men and women who make the things we need and who also talk to us in our own tongue about the things with which for the greater part of our lives we concern ourselves. Food, clothes, furniture, the whole apparatus of that world in which we live and move—but have not all our being.

The Visionaries

For we may in a moment be called away from all these familiar things to some saying of the remote past, to some work of that past and of a far distant country, to a Chinese poem or a Greek temple, to a text from the Gospel of St. John, or a phrase of Plotinus. We may know nothing about the Chinese ; we may never have heard of Plotinus ; the Gospel of St. John may be something which we expect to be read in church ; and yet suddenly, no matter how ignorant or hand-to-mouth we be, we are aware of this implication, preserved through the ages and yet fresh in our own minds. It is what makes these far distant speakers or makers friends to us, intimate as we are sometimes intimate for a moment with the best living human beings, or with ourselves when we think and feel deeply. And in this momentary intimacy we know a happiness often curiously compounded of other feelings, joy and grief, which we value for some reason above the most intense of our common pleasures. It may not be very intense itself. We may even be pained by the faintness with which we enjoy it ; but it represents for us a much intenser happiness, having no limits of time or intensity, which we might enjoy if we were equal to it. The experience of it is a moment perhaps, but one that takes us out of our routine hand-to-mouth existence, changes the aspect and meaning of all things for us, makes us serious and yet light-hearted, pains us, if at all, only because we feel our own inadequacy to it and know that in a moment we shall slip back into the life of use and wont. I may go into a great cathedral, or read this Chinese poem:

A poor man determines to go out into the world and make his fortune; his wife tries to detain him.

There was not a peck of rice in the bin:
There was not a coat hanging on the pegs,
So I took my sword and went towards the gate.
My wife and child clutched at my coat and wept:
" Some people want to be rich and grand:
I only want to share my porridge with you;
Above we have the blue waves of the sky;
Below the yellow face of this little child." [1]

Or this sentence of Plotinus:

" For the absolute good is the cause and source of all beauty, just as the sun is the source of all daylight, and it cannot therefore be spoken or written; yet we speak and write of it, in order to start and escort ourselves on the way and arouse our minds to the vision; like as when one showeth a pilgrim on his way to some shrine that he would visit: for the teaching is only of whither and how to go, the vision itself is the work of him who hath willed to see. [2]

All these things of whatever kind are not things I can enjoy like a glass of port. I can-

[1] *The Eastern Gate.* Anon. (First century B.C.). Translated by Arthur Waley, 170 *Chinese Poems*, p. 34.
[2] *Plotinus.* Paraphrased by Robert Bridges. "The Spirit of Man." Extract 69.

not draw the cork and hold the wine up to the light and smack my lips ; nor is it a question always whether I myself am equal to the experience of them. They are voices speaking for ever—sweet everlasting voices to which I am usually deaf ; nor is the pleasure, if it be pleasure that I get from them, only what is commonly called æsthetic or artistic,—at least if that is considered only as a part of the luxury or diversion of life. While I know it is reality itself, to which I may be unequal, compared with which I may be unreal ; and it may express the most poignant grief, as it does in the woman's answer in the Chinese poem above so that, unless I too am capable of such grief, I cannot experience it ; and always it has, with all its diversity of content or exterior purpose, an air of being withdrawn from my ordinary life so that I must free myself of that life to experience it. It may seem itself gay, light-hearted, like a slight poem by Prior or a *fête galante* by Watteau, but I must cast off use and wont to be aware what it says. I must consent to the implication of it ; and however gay it seems, there is a kind of seriousness in it, as of one who says what he means always and in the depth of his mind, even though he says it in the colour of a pot, or in the curves which he cuts upon it. These also

3   5

solemnize me, make me aware of an inner self which usually I forget, force from me an answer which surprises me, and which I too cannot put in words, yet it is a self compared with which my life of use and wont is mere habit and mechanism.

And yet this thing implied is always implied and not said. All through the ages there seems to be a reticence about it; or rather it is something so real and deep that men do not say it when it moves them, but say or do other things that are invested with its seriousness, reality, beauty, happiness. And whatever is done seriously or permanently and lacks it, irks us and discomforts us, as if it were a denial of something which we must believe even though we cannot say it, and as if by this implied denial it made us doubt that which we must believe to live at all. The intense seriousness and industry of the successful man of the world irks us so, or that of a whole modern city, occupied with hand-to-mouth tasks as if they were eternal; its threatening, inexpressive energy, or the remorseless accomplishment of art which has not that implication—these things distress us, even if we admire them. They rob us of vitality and make the self in us or other men seem insignificant: make what we value seem valueless to us. And still what is implied is not said, and where it fails to be implied, it is not denied. But still we feel its presence or absence. What is it ?

One cannot approach it without this curious reticence, without a kind of half unconscious inhibition which all through the ages has worked, producing the affirmation without words and without a statement of what is denied. And one reason for this inhibition is clear ; for that which is implied is itself so contrary to our ordinary hand-to-mouth experience and to our own routine way of living that we are afraid and almost ashamed to say it. How can we say it without insincerity, when, if it were true, it would make us live utterly differently, and yet we live as we do ? We are all filled with a natural shame, we tremble like a guilty thing surprised at every whisper of the deeper self, because it whispers so seldom ; and, when it does, we pay so little heed to it. And how can we pay more heed to it when we have our living to earn in a world of trivial struggle for life ? We may be sentimentalists, but there is all the same some kind of sincerity in us all. Since we live and must live in a certain way, we will not affirm that this life is wrong or meaningless. We have to establish a *modus vivendi*. When people tell us to leave father and mother and follow this implication, we may admire them, but we know that we cannot leave father and mother and husband

and wife and the rest of it. Therefore we leave
the implication merely implied, and will not
state it so that we may look it in the face. We
know that we shall not, we cannot, live according to it; and nothing would be more intolerable than a universe in which the truth would
be something on which we could not act. We
have a wholesome dislike to the people who tell
us that the truth is something on which we
cannot act and then revile us for not acting on
it. It were better that a millstone were hung
about their necks and they were cast into the
sea. For they are stumbling-blocks in the
difficult way of all us children; and the way
anyhow is difficult enough even if we do not
know where it is taking us.

Still I shrink from stating the implication;
yet I must state it if this book is to be written,
and I had better do so now lest the reader
become impatient. I shall no doubt fail to
state it quite right, and I must state it in several
propositions, confessing that I do but half believe it. For if I could believe it fully now and
always I should not be writing as I am, but
like the genius I should be, making shapes of
beauty for all time; I should be one of those
whom all men recognize as a friend, one of the
great visionaries, who are the despair and
delight of mankind.

It begins thus—whatever we value utterly

The Visionaries

and believe utterly with the whole of ourselves, no matter how rare or momentary that belief and value may be, that is the truth : not some one particular truth, but the truth about the whole nature of things ; and so the nature of things is not what it seems to us in our routine lives, but is the best possible, the best that we can imagine and far better, since the imagining of each one is lessened and limited by his particular weakness of feeling, of thought, of conduct. This best possible is something which the collective mind of man through the ages is trying to imagine, and that effort is a collective effort to conceive the truth.

Some visionaries have said this in one way, some in another, and that is the reason why they allure us. Laotze says it. Christ says it, especially in the Prodigal Son ; and Blake, too, says it. They say it in different ways, because each one of them is an individual in so far as he is real, and to each one there is an individual way of saying it. Christ, for instance, has his individual excellence, his own intensity of feeling, just as he has his own body and convolutions of the brain. To him the best possible means a God who loves, no matter what we do. A God who is like men when they shed happy tears, not over their own goodness, but over the deliverance of those they love. To Christ that God—how unlike the gods men worship—is the very nature of the universe, and all we have to do is to see him and by seeing to be constrained to act like him. He is not law or justice or system or will even; He is affection. To Christ the best possible is a nature of things, a reality, utterly human and personal, what we in our real and deeper selves value in human conduct. And Christ had no reason whatever for proclaiming this to be the truth except that it was what he valued, and what in the intensity of value he believed to be the truth behind the routine world, behind scribes and Pharisees and the Roman Empire and the huge menacing universe of things, behind life and death, pain and disease, behind the struggle of all things to go on living, behind their fears and hopes of a day. Behind it all there was this God who would not let a sparrow fall to the ground without being himself with it and of it. An absurd desperate affirmation, contrary to every item of our routine experience. An affirmation that provokes us, even while it allures; for, if it were true, why do we live always as if it were not? why are we, after millions of years of human effort, having risen from flint implements to aeroplanes, after miracles of human skill and wisdom, utterly unconvinced of its truth, so that we still live in the routine world and have our investments, our armaments and our whole system of de-

fences against nature and each other ? Why do
we go mad and suffer tortures and torture each
other ? This God must either be a figment or
an absurd futile being, a contradiction in terms.

I am not attempting satire. I am weary of
it and of all denunciations of the human race.
I write in a mood of weariness, and I cannot
believe, I am even distressed by the words
" Come unto me all ye that labour and are
heavy laden." They are printed words to me,
repeated by men who know no more than I do.
I do not see this God anywhere, and, though I
might wish to believe in him so that I might
have rest in illusion, I cannot.

*   *   *   *   *

But I cannot leave the matter thus. Like
all men nowadays who think at all about the
nature of things, I am troubled by what seems
to be a growing discrepancy between the facts
of the external world discovered by science, or
even some of the facts of the human mind discovered by the new science of psychology, and
certain beliefs achieved in the past by religion
and philosophy without which a rational happiness appears to be impossible. In a convenient
phrase it is a discrepancy between judgments
of fact and judgments of value. A judgment
of fact says, " This is so "; a judgment of
value says, " This ought to be so "; but what

is very often seems to us very different from what ought to be.

It is often said that the discrepancy between judgments of fact and judgments of value is simply a discrepancy between what is true and what we wish to believe; but that I think is in two respects unjust to judgments of value. For, in the first place, judgments of value are not to those who make them merely the expression of a wish. They may even be contrary to some particular and pressing desire of the moment. They seem to us all, when we make them, rather the expression of a universal and permanent state of mind to which we ourselves are but imperfectly subject. We may rebel against it or be false to it, but we recognize the difference, in ourselves and in others, between it and all desires which do not express it. In abstract terms we express it when we say that truth is better than falsehood, righteousness than unrighteousness, beauty than ugliness; but this abstract expression is based on a concrete experience. It is because we have known particular truths and falsehoods, actual righteous and unrighteous conduct, actual things beautiful and ugly, that we make the general statement; and the judgment of value is always, to begin with, a judgment of particulars, though in religion and philosophy it rises to a statement of faith. This statement of faith is not shaken by the fact that our judgment in particulars may often be mistaken. We know that we ourselves do but imperfectly obey and express the universal and permanent will ; but we keep the desire to obey and express it more perfectly. No one I think really believes that the difference between righteousness and un-righteousness, truth and falsehood, beauty and ugliness, is a matter of circumstance or taste. Some may from despondency or perversity pro-fess to believe that; but they will not act on their professed belief. Say what they will, they are surprised into judgments of value in which the whole self speaks with an unconscious conviction, stronger than any argument they may advance against it.

And this brings me to my second point against those who depreciate judgments of value. They forget in their worship of facts that judgments of value are facts—of the human mind. If we value righteousness, truth and beauty, as we become aware of them in concrete instances, more than bare success in the struggle for life ; if we are troubled when we do not act on that value ; if all that we call education, religion, philosophy, does in the main aim at the increase, strengthening and clarifying of that value, and the acting upon it—then there must be something in the nature of ourselves, in the nature of the universe even, which produces that value and intensifies it through the course of human experience. Granted a discrepancy, it is not merely between fact and human illusion but between the facts of reality and the facts of the human mind. If our judgments of value were mere illusion, we might expect that with greater knowledge and experience of external reality we should subject our judgments of value to that reality. But that is not what happens. However firmly we may be convinced by the discoveries of science that there is no righteousness in the universe outside the human mind, we are not also convinced that righteousness is not righteousness. There may be no love in the struggle for life as it is observed by biologists, but that does not lessen their value for love in St. Paul's sense of the word. No theory of evolution will make us prefer a millionaire to St. Francis or Christ. Rather the judgment of value rises defiant and despairing against the judgment of fact. It is, with the change only of a few terms, the defiance of the great chorus in *Atalanta* :

Because thou art over all who are over us ;
Because thy name is life and our name death ;
Because thou art cruel and men are piteous,
And our hands labour and thine hand scattereth,
Lo, with hearts rent and knees made tremulous,
Lo, with ephemeral lips and casual breath,
At least we witness of thee ere we die

The Visionaries

That these things are not otherwise, but thus,
That each man in his heart sigheth and saith,
That all men even as I,
All we are against thee, against thee, O God most
high.

And, if we read Euripides, we see that this sense of discrepancy, this defiance is not new. Science has only connected and systematized the facts which do violence to the human conscience. Religion has often been false to itself in attempting to subject the human conscience to those facts. It has justified the ways of God to man, when those ways were evil according to the judgment of man. Hence the revolt against religion, against the gods, against God. Always, finally, that is a revolt of judgments of value against the effort to subject them to judgments of fact. The militant atheist denies God because, according to the facts of the universe as he sees them, there cannot be a good God. To him it seems that the belief in God is an attempt to justify and glorify the facts of the universe; and he would rather defy those facts with the facts of his own mind, that is, with his judgments of value.

Nietzsche in *Beyond Good and Evil*[1] has a passage at once profound and perverse upon man's religious cruelty to himself.

[1] *Beyond Good and Evil*, translated by Helen Zimmern, pp. 73–4. T. N. Foulis. 1909.

15

" Once," he says, " men sacrificed human beings to their God. Then, during the moral epoch of mankind, they sacrificed to their God the strongest instincts in their nature. Finally, what still remained to be sacrificed ? Was it not necessary in the end for men to sacrifice everything comforting, holy, healing— all hope, all faith in hidden harmonies, in future blessedness and justice ? Was it not necessary to sacrifice God Himself, and out of cruelty to themselves to worship stone, stupidity, gravity, fate, nothingness ? " Nietzsche does not see the secret of this continuing and progressive " religious cruelty." It is the conflict between judgments of fact and judgments of value, and the effort and refusal to subject the latter to the former. The facts seem cruel and religion preaches submission to them, even worship of them in the form of a cruel God. The God becomes incredible through judgments of value, and then there follows a worship, as Nietzsche puts it, of stone, stupidity, gravity, fate, nothingness, which again is an effort to submit judgments of value to judgments of fact. Against this worship Nietzsche revolts with his own judgments of value. All his philosophy is such a revolt, defiant and despairing ; for he cannot find that which he would worship according to his own judgments of value, and his overman is but another idol, set up somewhere in the future.

But Nietzsche proves as clearly as any man that judgments of value are permanent facts of the human mind from which it cannot escape. Least of all do those escape from it who attack our judgments of value as mere attempts to escape from the bitter truth. For if the truth is bitter, why should we *not* try to escape from it ? If the universe is a cruel practical joke, made by nobody, why not baffle the non-existent joker, by believing that it is other than it is ? Why has the complete sceptic this scorn of illusion, unless it be that he values truth at all costs ? That is the deep unconscious inconsistency of his position. Condemning all our values as delusions, he still preserves, as an unexamined dogma, his own value for truth. That judgment of value is what impels him to condemn other judgments of value; but why should he value truth at all, if the universe be what he maintains it to be ? He may assert that truth is always useful, but that is mere assertion. Nothing is so well worth having, even materially, as happiness, and in a universe of nonsense we are more likely to be happy if we believe lies about it than if we believe the truth. In fact a lie may have more " survival value " than the truth if it gives us conviction and vitality. In a universe of illusion let us choose those illusions which are most comforting; let us accept the doctrine of Retting in *The Wild Duck* and persuade ourselves by auto-suggestion to believe what we will.

But that we do not do.

* * * * *

The Religion of the Particular ◠

WE are all aware of two different ways in which we can regard things and people; one in which they are members of some class to us, the other in which they are individuals. This difference is not usually willed or conscious, and we turn from the one way to the other according to the needs of the moment. We may think of classification as a scientific process, and it is one consciously used by science; but men must have always classified. A savage, for instance, will see the members of his own family as individuals, but the members of another tribe as members of that tribe. And he will classify things as soon as he begins to make use of them. Flints, for instance, to palæolithic man were the kind of stone out of which weapons or tools could be best made; but when he had made a tool out of flint, it would become his individual tool in which he had a right of property and in which he took some pride.

So classification is natural to man, and the

classifications of science have grown out of primitive classifications of utility. Science, like the savage, classifies with a purpose, though its purpose may be pure knowledge. But the classifications of science, unlike those of the savage, have always a most valuable result ; namely the withdrawal of the objects classified from all emotional associations, even if those objects be human beings. Thus, when the savage saw a certain number of men as members of another tribe, he often, because of this very classification, felt an emotion of violent hostility to them ; but when science observes criminals as a class, they are not wicked men to it but men so classified with the object of learning more about them. They are no longer bad or good in themselves but objects about which knowledge is desired.

The impartiality of science, though intellectual rather than moral in its purpose, has the noblest moral effects and is one of the highest achievements of man. Slowly and imperfectly it has spread from the contemplation and treatment of things to the contemplation and treatment of persons. Slowly we are learning to disdain, even in ourselves, those primitive partialities which put on a moral disguise to pervert justice. It is science which has taught us to classify, not for the purposes of feud and contempt, but for the purposes of knowledge, to observe differences rather than to resent them. It is science which dethrones the Ego, whether individual or national, from its seat of absolute judgment. It is still natural in us to think that my country must be right in all things because it is my country ; but science makes us aware of that tendency, tells us that in it also the wish is father to the thought, and teaches us, by the analogy of all its achievements, to purge thought of the wish, so that it may be thought indeed, and not instinct rationalized. Power is to be won, it assures us, by consenting to truth, by seeing all things as they are, not as we wish them to be. So science has its own faith and even its own religion.

It may seem a cold religion, but it has moved great men to great emotions. In the Note Books of Leonardo are hymns to Necessity and the reign of Law—" O marvellous Necessity, thou with supreme reason constrainest all effects to be the direct results of their causes, and by a supreme and irrevocable law every natural action obeys thee by the shortest possible process."[1] To Leonardo, at that moment of time, the sense of necessity meant not tyranny but freedom : the delivery of man's mind from its own enslaving phantasies about the universe, from its own vain but mischievous

[1] From Leonardo da Vinci's Note Books, E. McCurdy.

efforts to evade law, and from magic and superstition and myth pretending to be knowledge.
It must have been to him as if the windows of
the world were suddenly opened and everything
purged, by a fresh wind, of an unpleasant human
smell. For it is science and that alone which
can teach men to detect and to dislike that close
human smell in his beliefs. Further, for Leonardo as for the Stoics, the words " In harmony " were not meaningless or even cold. He
believed that behind the transitory will of the
Ego there is a universal will which each man
may discover to be his own, if only he will
submit himself to it, not passively, but by the
active process of discovery. " Falsehood," he
said, " is so vile that, though it should praise
the works of God, it offends against His divinity ; truth is of such excellence that if it praise
the meanest things they become ennobled."
But truth is always something to be discovered
or recognized ; and this discovery or eager
recognition was his way of worship.

We can understand how Leonardo could be
satisfied with that way of worship at that
moment of time ; but it will not satisfy men
always, and does not satisfy them now. We are
used to the idea of necessity, and it does not
seem to us altogether divine ; we are used to
the process of discovery, and we ask something
more of the universe than that we should have

The Religion of the Particular

an infinite capacity of exploring it. We may
be told that this demand for something more is
unreasonable, but still we make it ; and still we
hope that there is a further and a different kind
of truth which our process of discovery does not
tell us.

This further truth, if it exists, cannot be found
by repudiating truths already discovered ; but
it may be that it awaits its own method of discovery, that the method of science, too exclu-
sively followed or even mis-applied, may be
now misleading us about the most important
truths of all. It may be that the method of
classification brings its own illusions with it
against which we need to be set on our guard.

Of the value of that method and its great
achievements I have already spoken. Its
danger begins when we forget that it is process
applied by the human mind, when we slip into
the illusion that it is, as it were, applied by
nature herself, and promising us the complete
and ultimate truth about everything. That is
a metaphysical assumption not made or needed
by the method itself ; but we slip into it more
easily because we associate the process with
the scientific process and all its achievements.
Since we have acquired so much knowledge
by means of classification, and freed ourselves
from much error, we are apt to believe that
reality itself consists in classification, or, to put

it more precisely, that the nature of things and of people lies in what they have in common, not in their peculiarities. Classification means the discovery of common qualities and the insistence on them ; it does not mean that they are the only qualities or that other qualities have no significance. Thus mathematics is the science in which classification is carried furthest, which postulates as it were a whole universe of its own for purposes of classification, in which all things exist by reason of their common qualities or differences and in which nothing has any value except for the purposes of science. But mathematics does not assert that this universe of its own is the only universe or that the whole truth about an isosceles triangle is the same, or of the same nature, as the whole truth about man. It is concerned, not with metaphysics, but with its own business ; and, if its abstracting habit invades the whole mind of a particular mathematician—if it causes him, in his politics, for instance, to regard men as if they were isosceles triangles— that is a case of trade disease, not of philosophic conviction.

We can see the absurdity of regarding men politically as if they were isosceles triangles, because politics have an immediate practical effect on our lives. Still more clearly do we see the absurdity of regarding them so in our

The Religion of the Particular

personal relations with them, because these relations have a still closer practical effect on our lives. The men and women we live and work with are to us individuals and arouse in us, as individuals, a set of emotions different in kind from those aroused in the most passionate mathematician by the most interesting problem. And the difference is this : that, while the mathematician cannot value an isosceles triangle in itself, however much he may value the discovery of mathematical truth, we value individuals in themselves and as individuals ; and a great part, the greater part, of our life and conduct is controlled by these values. A man's wife is to him herself, not a member of the class of wives. If, for some reason, he turns to considering her as a member of the class of wives—that is to say, scientifically—he must, for the purpose of that consideration, empty her of all her peculiar qualities and, with them, he must empty his mind of its peculiar value of her. When she enters the class of wives she drops for the moment all that he means when he thinks of her as his wife. So, if he thought of her always as a member of the class of wives, she would cease to be his wife to him and would become what a plant is to a botanist when he is regarding it as a member of a species. In that case he would not be a satisfactory husband. We do not consider that men ought to empty their wives of content so that they may consider them scientifically, precisely because the relation between husband and wife is more real and important than any scientific process. We should even go so far as to say that a man who thus sacrifices his married life to a scientific process could know little of wives or of anything else worth knowing.

Yet, though in practice we thus refuse to empty wives and other human beings of their content for scientific purposes, in theory we believe that to do that to all things is the only way of reaching the truth about the nature of the universe. The botanist, when he considers a plant as the member of a species, does, quite rightly, empty it of its beauty and of all the emotions which that beauty may arouse in him.

> A primrose by the river's brim
> A yellow primrose is to him
> And it is nothing more—

Not because, like Peter Bell, he is without a sense of beauty or of anything except utility, but because he is considering the common qualities of the species and not the peculiarities of any particular primrose. But, when we see a primrose as a beautiful thing, it is that particular primrose we see in that particular spot at that particular moment. In fact, it has a reality for us as an individual which disappears when we consider it as a member of a species;

The Religion of the Particular

and the emotion of value aroused by its beauty in us is aroused in us by the individual not by the species. So a man's emotion of value for his wife is aroused and maintained by her as an individual behaving in a particular way at particular moments ; it is not aroused by the thought of her as a member of the class of wives or of women or of any other class. And this emotion of value roused by a human being, or a plant, or anything else, gives us a sense of the reality of the individual and of its peculiar qualities which most powerfully affects our conduct, but which yet we are apt to ignore in our theories of the nature of the universe.

For in those theories we do more and more assume that there is nothing in the universe, in particular things, which arouses our sense of value. We believe, and are made unhappy by that belief, that our values are entirely and unaccountably contributed by ourselves. Beauty, for instance, is something, not in the nature of things, but only in our nature. When we see it we make it. We have the pathetic power of loving, and we value that power above all things. But outside ourselves there is nothing lovable ; and now we begin to tell ourselves that within ourselves there is nothing lovable either. Below our consciousness, with its illusion of peculiarities in ourselves and in others, there is an unconscious consisting only of

common qualities, or as we call them instincts,
forces, which no one who was aware of them
could love any more than we can love the
attraction of gravity. It is the consciousness
with its illusion of peculiarities which not only
makes love, but also makes what is lovable. A
man's wife may be his wife to his consciousness ;
but the reality lies in an unconscious in both of
them which is merely generic and so incapable
of valuing or of being valued.

This, of course, is a monstrous belief to us in
practice and cannot affect our conduct. Yet
we have a fear that it may be true all the same :
that there is a nightmare incongruity between
the universe of our values and the universe of
fact, that if we knew the truth about all things
we should be incapable of love and so incapable
of life.

It is only lately that our habit of what I call
the illusion of classification has invaded our
thought about ourselves. But that invasion
one can see now was bound to happen ; if the
reality of things consists only of their common
qualities, if there is nothing in them which
arouses our emotions of value and those emotions with their causes are entirely contributed
by us, then what is sauce for the goose is sauce
for the gander, what is true of things is true of
man himself. The emotion of value gives us an
illusion of the reality of the particular in the

The Religion of the Particular

primrose ; it also gives us an illusion of the reality of the particular in the wife. She too, if we could know the very pulse of the machine in the unconscious ; would be merely generic, a machine driven by instincts which in themselves no one could value, because they are merely common qualities diversely combined in different machines.

In practice, of course, most of us do escape from this nightmare ; but practice is not enough. We have a religion of love still ; but it will grow weaker and weaker if we are forced to believe that it is solely our own creation with no corresponding reality outside us. But what is it that forces us to believe that ? Why should we assume that reality is to be found in things only when they are classified, and so emptied of their value for us ? The answer, I think, is to be found in history, not in reason. Since by classification we discover certain truths, since science has by means of it freed us from so much superstition and prejudice and egotism, we have come to believe that it tells us, not only the truth and nothing but the truth, but also the whole truth.

Yet in fact we are constantly aware of another kind of knowledge, not discovered by classification and not only of common qualities, in which we firmly believe and upon which we act. This is a knowledge of particular persons

and things : a knowledge in which they are not
analysed to discover what they have in common
with other persons and things of the same kind,
but in which they are seen as units, as separate
and coherent wholes whose reality consists in
their unity, identity, coherence. This kind of
knowledge is often called intuitive, a term used
by some to glorify and by others to depreciate
it ; it might better perhaps be called emotional
knowledge, since it is gained through the
emotions and not through their elimination.
It is most signally displayed in art ; and the
difference between art and science is the difference between these two kinds of knowledge.

These two human activities do not compete
or conflict with each other, so that there is no
superiority or inferiority in either of them.
The artist cannot tell us what the man of
science tells us ; but it is necessary to insist
now that there is a knowledge proper to art as
to science. It is often said, for instance, that
Shakespeare has a great knowledge ; of the
human heart ; but that is not scientific or
psychological or general knowledge ; it is not a
knowledge of qualities common to classes of
human beings, but a knowledge of individual
characters obtained by emotional experience of
them ; and it is expressed and communicated,
not in scientific statement but in drama, that is
to say, in individuals both powerfully moved

The Religion of the Particular

by emotions and, what is more, emotionally presented by the dramatist. In his poetry Shakespeare contributes the events of his own mind also ; and these are his own emotional experiences, not merely the passions or qualities of human beings, but of human beings themselves seen in their identity and intense particularity. Hamlet is not a type but an individual ; and just because he is an individual, very sharply differentiated from other individuals, he is a masterpiece. We are amazed at the knowledge implied in him, and we know that it is not knowledge gained by mere observation, but rather by emotional experience of actual human beings. We know that Shakespeare could not have drawn him, if his interest in men had been purely scientific ; it must have been in itself an emotional interest aroused by individuals, not by classes and types.

And his presentation has, besides the delight we get from it, this added value for us, that it does convince us of the existence and validity of intuitive or emotional knowledge. That is what Keats perhaps meant when he said that beauty is truth, truth beauty. There is a truth of art arising through the emotional experience of the particular which must be presented emotionally by the artist—that is to say, in terms of beauty ; and in all great art we are convinced of truth through beauty and our delight is in the recognition of both as one in the work of art. This is not only true where human beings are concerned. When a great Chinese artist paints a lotus we have the same sense of emotional knowledge as in Hamlet. He has achieved it through his passion for the particular and what he gives us is the particular, that flower at that moment and no other. So it is with landscape; a great landscape is one particular scene at one particular moment painted in one particular way; and the particularity, the difference from all other works of the same kind, is what convinces and delights us. The artist may not paint any particular actual scene, as the dramatist may not draw an actual character; but both create out of their sense and value for particulars; they could not do it by classification or a scientific interest in common qualities.

There is indeed art, such as the art of music, in which the particularity seems to consist only in the work of art itself and not in anything represented by it—a point never made by musical critics. Yet music too arises out of the experience and value of the particular. We enjoy it, indeed, because it is charged with the values of the artist and communicates them to us. We have a sense of truth in great music, as of something won from actual experience; and the lack of that sense bad in music, which may

The Religion of the Particular

please us at first but afterwards seems to empty itself of content, to be generalized and like much other music. Nothing is so fatal to any work of art as that it should become one of a class to us. That is why all textbooks that classify works of art as classical or romantic, as impressionist or post-impressionist or what not, seem to rob them of all the art in them ; for if a work of art can be classified, it lacks the particularity of art. Hamlet is not classical or romantic, it is Hamlet. Generalized art in fact is a contradiction in terms, for the very material of art is knowledge of the particular and its virtue consists in its own particularity.

Now the emotion expressed in art is always finally the emotion of value—though this may be contrasted with and heightened by the contrary emotion, as when we have Cordelia and Goneril in the same play. Without values there could be no art ; for the beauty of art is itself the expression of value and the communication of it. That again is where it differs both in content and in form from science, which, not being concerned with values, is not concerned with beauty of expression—at least, where the man of science is concerned with beauty of expression, he is also concerned with values and is becoming an artist. A mathematician, for instance, may speak with delight of the beauty of some solution ; but that is because he values beauty, at least of form, and so delights in the intense particularity of that solution. It has become to him what a flower is to an artist. But emotion of value is always for the parti-cular. We have of course values on principle, as where we say that we value truth or that we ought to be lovers of human kind. But these are based on emotions of value for the parti-cular. We could not even wish to love our kind unless we had loved individual men and women ; we could not love truth unless we had been delighted with the recognition or dis-covery of particular truths. There indeed is common ground between science and art ; and the explanation of the fact is that some part of the process of scientific discovery seems to be artistic and intuitive. The great discoverer is, as it were, stung by the sudden glory of truth and a particular truth ; and his desire then is to expose that truth in all its particularity, as Michelangelo desired to expose a particular figure in marble. He differs from the artist in that his subject-matter is the general : but his treatment of it, like the artist's, is particular ; and, like him, he is urged on towards perfection of statement by the emotion of value. That emotion brings into play these intuitive facul-ties which are supposed to be proper to art, and which therefore are supposed by many to be merely æsthetic and concerned with myth or fiction rather than with fact.

Now it is always very difficult, sometimes impossible, to express intuitive knowledge in intellectual, or, as Croce would say, in conceptual terms. It is the kind of knowledge that we act on rather than formulate. We attain, for instance, in some moment of strong and shared emotion, to an intuitive knowledge of a man's character. He has, as we say, revealed himself to us ; from that moment he is utterly a friend for ever, and we know we can trust him. That is a knowledge we will act on; but we cannot formulate it except in vague terms. Yet we are sure that it is knowledge ; and it is difficult to formulate just because it is knowledge of the particular, of one individual man who is a living coherent whole to us. That very knowledge prevents us from classifying him, for the better we know him the more unique he is to us. The only way to communicate our knowledge of him would be the artistic, to present him in all his intense particularity in some form of art. That probably we cannot do ; yet the knowledge remains knowledge because we can act on it, because, as we say, we know what he will do without possibility of our being deceived.

But that is only one example of intuitive knowledge and of the difficulty of formulating it. Always we are acquiring knowledge, intuitive knowledge, through the emotion of value ; always there is the same difficulty of expressing it in intellectual or conceptual terms. It is this difficulty which causes the huge discrepancy between the conduct and emotions on one hand, and the formulated beliefs on the other, for many men of high intelligence. There is a real conflict which causes them real anguish between that intuitive knowledge obtained through the emotion of value—that knowledge of the coherent and living and particular upon which they act—and their own scientific knowledge, obtained by the process of classification and a concern with generalities emptied of values, upon which they form their theories of the nature of things. It is natural and easy to act on intuitive knowledge, when you love men, to trust them ; and it is natural and easy to turn scientific knowledge into theories. But to formulate theories out of intuitive knowledge is hard ; and to act on the theories formulated out of scientific knowledge is often happily impossible.

Yet the great philosopher is he who is not content with theories based on any scientific knowledge, theories on which neither he nor anyone else will act; theories which leave a gulf between judgments of act and judgments of value. The very problem of philosophy for him is the problem of making concepts also out

of intuitive knowledge, of not leaving its
expression to art and myth alone. He knows
that philosophy must be based on experience
and that our experience is not only of things
classified by their common qualities and so
emptied of values. On one side the universe,
when we observe it for certain practical purposes, may seem a mechanism of generalized
processes ; but those processes are for those
practical purposes emptied of a great part of
our experience and also of a great part of our
knowledge. When we think of those processes
as the whole truth, then the universe does
indeed seem to us something meaningless and
irresponsive, and we cry that, for all our love of
nature, nature will not return our love. Then
it seems to us that man is a lonely artist in
space wasting his sweetness on the desert air,
something irrationally and pathetically unique,
with no value or purpose in his uniqueness,
since he has become what he is in a universe
without value or purpose. But processes are
not the whole truth, and if we expect them to
satisfy our values or to answer to the artist
and the lover that is in us, we shall certainly be
disappointed. Besides the genera of flowers
there is always the particular flower, the primrose by the river's brim ; and it is ungrateful
to lament that it says nothing to us. It does
speak to us in its beauty, just as individual

human beings speak to us in all that we find to
love in them. The whole about them we know
is not in their common qualities, in psychological generalities emptied of value ; it is also in
their individuality, their uniqueness, that
which we love in them. Why then is not also
some part of the truth about the universe in
the individuality, the uniqueness, the beauty of
things, and why do we call that beauty irresponsive ? It has not our speech, but it is
speaking to us always, just as human works of
art speak to us. And our art is not a despairing
cry into an empty void, but rather an answer to
all the speaking beauty of the universe.

You may say all this is mere sentiment and
rhetoric. A primrose is not aware of my
existence or indeed of anything, and the stars,
whatever the poets may say about them, are
merely lumps of blind matter subject to blind
forces. Yet beauty is a fact for us, just as all
that we love in human beings is a fact for us.
Even if you say it is a fact made by our minds,
yet our minds which make it are a part of the
universe. And what precisely do you mean, if
you say it is made by our minds ? It is not a
delusion of disordered minds or a theory that
may be false, but an experience that happens
to us as normally and constantly as our experiences of natural phenomena. True, some men
see beauty where others do not. There is a

sense in which the human mind makes truth, but
not without any correspondence or contact with
external reality; and in just the same sense,
and with the same correspondence, the human
mind makes beauty. There is no beauty in
the primrose to Peter Bell, there was beauty in
it to Wordsworth; but will anyone pretend
that Wordsworth was subject to a delusion
from which Bell was free, or that Wordsworth
achieved a private beauty of the primrose for
his particular self? The mere fact of art disproves that; for it implies a common sense of
beauty and of all values, without which the
artist would be always talking only to himself.

In some sense beauty is a fact of the universe
as it is of our minds. In the case of art we know
that it has an existence independent of us.
However true it may be that the colours of a
picture exist only in the eye and the sound of
music in the ear, yet there is an artist speaking
to others through the sound and colour. All our
views about the nature of the universe must be
drawn from the whole of our experiences. Yet
we must have them; for if we do not reach
them consciously, we shall reach them unconsciously, and be at the mercy of digestion or
private fortune. Some, therefore, have said
that we should believe what will best help us to
life. Nietzsche said that we cannot help
doing that, that all belief is an expression of the

will to power. But the very determination to believe what will help you to live, or make you comfortable, is itself a despair about the nature of the universe; and comfort cannot be based on despair.

If we believe in the universe, we believe in a truth that can be more and more discovered and a truth that cannot be reduced into anything but itself. Indeed it is part of the purpose of every man's life to discover out of his own experience his own particularity of truth; because he is an individual with a unique experience, he can know something about the whole nature of things that no one else knows; and all truth attained by our own experience has this particularity in it, the character and the quality of the individual; as we know, whenever we come on an impassioned expression of such truth, it bears in its very expression marks of the passion and labour by which it was acquired.

Take for instance this passage from a sermon by John Donne on the Bounty of God:

If I should declare what God hath done (done occasionally) for my soule, where he instructed me for feare of falling, where he raised me when I was fallen, perchance you would rather fixe your thoughts upon my illnesse, and wonder at that, than at Gods goodnesse, and glorify him in that; rather wonder at my sins than at his mercies, rather consider how ill a man I was, than how good a God he is. If I should inquire

The Religion of the Particular

upon what occasion God elected me, and writ my name in the book of life, I should sooner be afraid that it were not so, than finde a reason why it should be so. God made sun and moon to distinguish seasons, and day, and night, and we cannot have the fruits of the earth but in their seasons : But God hath made no decree to distinguish the seasons of his mercies ; In Paradise, the fruits were ripe, the first minute, and in heaven it is alwaies Autumne, his mercies are ever in their maturity. We ask *panem quotidianum*, our daily bread, and God never says you should have come yesterday, he never says you must again to-morrow, but *to-day if you will heare his voice*, to-day he will heare you. If some king of the earth have so large an extent of Dominion, in North and South, as that he hath Winter and Summer together in his Dominions, so large an extent East and West, as that he hath day and night together in his Dominions, much more hath God mercy and judgement together : He brought light out of darknesse, not out of a lesser light ; he can bring thy Summer out of Winter, though thou have no Spring ; though in the wayes of fortune, or understanding, or conscience, thou have been benighted till now, wintred and frozen, clouded and eclypsed, damped and benummed, smothered and stupified till now, now God comes to thee, not as in the dawning of the day, not as in the bud of the spring, but as the sun at noon to illustrate all shadowes, as the sheaves in harvest to fill all penuries, all occasions invite his mercies, and all times are his seasons.

*   *   *   *   *

III

The Logic of God ❧ ❧ ❧

IT is a common error, in the discussion of difficult questions, to consider only two alternatives when it may be that both are false and that some third ignored possibility would lead to the truth. So, when we ask whether there is a God we usually think only of meaning—Is there the God of whom we have heard in Church? And those who cannot believe in this God refuse to believe in any. Often they are filled with resentment against this God, because he seems to them to fall short of what God would be if he existed. They quote statements about him in the Bible or the Prayer Book as a proof that God is not divine, when, at most they prove that this particular God is not divine and therefore is not the true God; or they tell us of the harm that has been done by believing in him and the qualities imputed to him, as a reason why we should not believe in any God, whereas, of course, it is only a reason why we should not believe in this God.

42

The Logic of God

Many patients have been killed by doctors in the past; but that is not a reason why we should not believe in medical science, for the science which kills is not science at all. But, in spite of its error and mischief there may yet be a science to be discovered. So even if many false Gods have been worshipped there may yet be a true one to be found.

But if there is a God you cannot reach belief in him by a wrong process. You may believe in a God, but it is some one else whom you call by the same name and some one who does not exist. The true God demands that you shall reach him by the right way, demands this of mankind, in the mass, as well as of individuals. The effort to find him is a universal one in which even those who honestly deny him take part. Unless behind the hymns and the raptures there is reason, they are sung to an idol.

But this process you must not be the slave of, lest you mistake it for reality itself. All our dialectic may be shattered by a fact; for you can use dialectic to prove almost anything, especially things which no one would ever think of acting upon. And if you trust entirely in the dialectic process, you will lose your way, and either give it up, and break into some tawdry imitation paradise of your own desire, or else go wandering for ever and proclaim that you have discovered the truth which is not worth discovering. The slaves of dialectic are those who believe in the perfection of their own mental mechanism, and also those for whom their premises have a much more precise meaning than they can have. They play, for instance, with the words predestination and free will without seeing that those terms are almost counters, or again that the term causation is almost a counter, and that all three words need to be enriched with a much more exact and full knowledge than we have at present. So, too, the word God may be almost a counter, and is to many theologians and atheists. The great visionaries, however, do not reach a belief in God by means of dialectic based upon any universally acknowledged facts. For them God exists to begin with and they enrich their idea of him out of their experience. You might call them pragmatists or any other name, but no name would exactly fit them. They have a sense of reality in which they trust and by which they live, and if they persuade us they are right it is by the beauty and passion of their life and speech. But most of us lack their genius; we do not see God and we have by some means to make up our minds whether or no we will believe in him. No one, I suppose, would rather believe in a

The Logic of God

meaningless universe than in a good God;
those who refuse to believe in him have good
but unwilling reasons of their own, and often
the God they have heard of is not good enough,
does in fact reduce himself to an absurdity
by his lack of goodness. He is rejected—and
with him all ideas of God and the very notion
of theism.

But there is, or is supposed to be, a science
of theology; by its name it professes to be a
science—and there' cannot be a human being
who does not wish it were one. A science that
would lead us to knowledge of, to close real
contact with, a supreme reality, a science, as
it must be if it is worth anything, that would
prove itself in some way out of our experience,
but still a science that anyone could learn and
practice, not the art of the mystics that
requires genius or lunacy. What a science
that would be, the mistress of all sciences
necessary to all men, the basis of all knowledge,
the science of direction of value, of uttermost
truth! But though we have the name, who
can say we have the thing?

Medical science is science, or is on the way
to being science, because the doctors, with all
their faults, do not say that it has all been
discovered. They may often be unscientific
in practice or bigoted against particular in-
novations, but they do not have a theory

45

which makes science impossible, they do not
say that Galen or even Jenner is infallible.
They do not force upon us the alternatives
that they are either infallible or quacks; and
if some treatment of theirs does kill patients
instead of curing them, they may for a time
conceal the fact, but they do, after a decent
interval, alter their treatment. Therefore we
do not either obey them as all infallible or
condemn them all as quacks. We know that
their science is a growing science, subject to
all the infirmities of the human mind but rich
with its promise.

But the doctors of theology have not escaped
from mediæval traditions. Theology is not
yet a science to them because, just as the
physicians of the Middle Ages were occupied
with Galen, so the theologians are occupied
with the Scriptures and with commentaries
upon them. For them there has been a
golden age of theology, when it was not science
but revelation; and so it is not a science to
them now. How then can it be a science to
others? The theologian does not contemplate
the possibility that God exists, but not his
God. He writes as the member of a Church,
usually as a priest or minister of some Christian
sect, and professionalism imposes certain
axioms upon him which he never questions.
Few laymen are theologians, and we can

scarcely imagine a theologian in Europe who
is not a Christian. Yet if theology were a
science, there would be no reason whatever
why a theologian should be a priest, a minister,
or even a Christian. The question whether
God exists and what is the nature of God is
one that concerns all men. Many Christians,
if they read this, will be startled by my suggestion that there has not been a golden age
of theology in the past, when it was revealed,
that theology can be regarded as a science
still in its infancy and as one which may have
to confess that it has hitherto made more
mistakes than discoveries. They will think
that my aim must be insidiously to destroy
all religion, all faith. To raise the question
whether there is a God and whether, if there is,
we have discovered anything about him, is to
them mere agnosticism. They are of one
party, the party that believes in one particular
God; and there is the other party which believes
that there is no such God; neither of these
parties will consider the existence of a third
party, or even of an individual, who would consider the question afresh, ask anew whether
there is a God, and what is his nature.

And yet, if God exists, it seems likely that we
ought to be even now in some way capable of
discovering his existence and of some facts
about his nature. If God exists he must be

alive. He must be the God of the living, not
of the dead, 'and himself a living God; but to
believers and unbelievers alike he is a God of
the past, and so theology is not a science nor
capable of becoming one. To the unbeliever
it is myth making, to the believer at most a
refinement or explanation of truths revealed
long ago. Pascal, for instance, speaking in his
Pensées of the misuse of authority in philosophy, says that ancient authors are authorities
upon matters of fact alone, and upon those
matters of fact which we can discover only
from them ; and then he distinguishes theology
from philosophy and science as being the kind
of knowledge in which authority is absolute.
For in theology authority is inseparable from
truth, which cannot be known without it.
To be certain about matters incomprehensible
to the reason we have only to see them stated
in the Scriptures. The principles of theology
are above nature and reason, and the mind
of man could not discover them by its own
efforts, they are revealed to us by an omnipotent and supernatural power.

Pascal himself was a man of science and
by nature sceptical he would have exercised
his scepticism upon theology if he had not
denied that it was a science. Claiming perfect
freedom for the mind in all sciences, he fears
that freedom in religion, and therefore sets it

above reason. Its facts are known by a process not scientific, and are therefore not subject to scientific processes. Pascal thought clearly on this matter. He said to his own exorbitant reason, Thus far and no farther. But his doctrine of the absolute authority of the Scriptures can be held by no one now. Even the Roman Catholic Church does more and more substitute its own authority for that of the Scriptures. And for those who are not Roman, science has undermined the authority of the Scriptures by a process unknown to and unimagined by Pascal. The very documents from which he derived all authority are questioned. And even those for whom Christ speaks absolute truth use the methods of science to discover what he said.

It is two hundred and fifty years since Pascal wrote, and theology is still not a science. Authority still lurks in it, even though the extent of that authority be not defined outside the Church of Rome.

Those to whom it is mythology say that, if theology were capable of being a science, it would have become one already, would have discovered some facts that no one could deny ; those to whom it is revelation say that these facts have been revealed. They are afraid of losing what they have got and, curiously, they do not believe in revelation now continuing and perhaps improving. What they have they preserve or embalm in their creeds against decay; they assume that the belief in God is fighting a losing battle—because there is none other that fighteth for us, but only thou, O God. Or rather because God himself does not fight for them, does not continue to reveal himself, but refers unbelievers back to what he has once said—he is not speaking now. Is it to be wondered at that believers and unbelievers take them at their word and refuse interest in this science of documents and scriptures? They prefer the science of experiment and discovery.

But in the effort to treat theology as a science we are faced by a difficulty which must be confessed at once. If God exists, he is the most important fact of the universe, a fact of which men must always consciously, or unconsciously, directly or indirectly, have been aware. He must have forced himself upon their attention as soon as they began to take notice of anything. Now certainly there have been Gods; most peoples have believed in a God so far back as we know anything of human history; but what divers and obviously absurd Gods most of them have believed in. Moloch, Baal, Juggernaut, Jupiter, Jahveh— these are no facts that have forced themselves upon the attention of mankind, they are

fables in which men have believed through
some perversity, the cause of which we do not
yet fully understand, and fables which have
made them blind, cruel, and unhappy. If God
is a fact, why has he led men into such errors
about himself, or why have they fallen into
such errors ? Why do they still fall into them ?
Can you wonder that men should cry *Écrasez
l'infame* ? It is the belief in a lie that has cost
us so much blood, so many tears ; let us escape
into the reality of a Godless universe !

Yes ; but, if there is the fact of God, there
is also the fact of man's nature and its liability
to error. Consider how, with the facts of the
human body to be discovered, doctors also
have caused so much blood-letting and so
many tears, how they too have pretended to
know what they did not know, how they have
sacrificed mankind to their profession and
themselves. All science is a rare and late
achievement, and yet it deals with facts that
were always there to be seen or discovered.
Always the progress of science was hindered
by the professional unconscious conspiracy to
maintain that the profession knows and can
tell the laity. So, if God is the most important
fact of all, we might expect the most powerful
profession to concern itself with him and the
most inveterate professional conspiracy to
conceal the truth about him ; and this is what

has happened. The other sciences have attained to some freedom because they concern themselves with immediate facts and can often be tested by immediate results ; but theology has not attained to that freedom because it is concerned with the ultimate fact and the one of most importance to mankind, so that mankind are at once made anxious about it with all their hopes and fears, yet unable to test any theories about it by immediate results. It is that branch of human inquiry most favourable to professional conspiracy and the branch which has accordingly produced the most powerful conspiracy, so powerful that its inquiry has not even yet begun to be a science.

But, you may well ask, granted all this, and granted the fact of God's existence—how can theology become a science ? Science is concerned with facts directly or indirectly perceived by the senses, and God, we are all agreed, cannot be perceived by the senses— no man hath seen God at any time. But there is one science not concerned with facts of sense —mathematics is concerned with numbers which we do not see as numbers, or with geometrical figures which we do not see as geometrical figures. It is a science made by the mind of man, the very subject matter of which is made by the mind of man and which is then applied to the facts of the human mind. No one concerns himself with the question whether or no numbers exist in the material world, though you may hold any mystical doctrine of their immaterial existence, but they are of use to man in his dealings with the material world. He makes certain postulates about them, or rather those postulates happen to his mind, and working upon those postulates he is able to discover many things of immediate use to himself. So theology, if it can be a science at all, must be one more like mathematics than, say, botany. It must concern itself with postulates that happen to the human mind and must endeavour to discover what are the postulates that do happen to the human mind with regard to God; having discovered them, it may find those postulates of use in the actual conditions of life.

In the past theology has not been so practised, because, unlike mathematics, it is concerned with a matter that inflames human passions, hopes and fears. In the past men have used the postulate of God's existence to explain the origin of things, to maintain their own superiority to other men, to satisfy their need of a supernatural enemy to their own natural foes, to give an undeniable authority to statements they wished to make (often statements of great and immediate social use), to be

6

a confidant, a lawgiver, even a tyrant, and a means of torturing them when they wished to torture themselves. God—the point is one we shall develop later—has always been an authority not to be questioned. He has given certainty on many points about which man wished for certainty but had not earned it; and he has of course played into the hands of particular classes or nations who wished to impose for their own purposes a certainty upon others.

So the postulate of God's existence has implied nothing about his nature except that he is more powerful than men. He is not necessarily omnipotent. His will may be frustrated by other gods, or by fate, but he is always powerful enough to act as a court of appeal from some men against others. He is the arbiter in disputes and an arbiter on the side of those who can by force impose their own beliefs about him; and they have imposed consciously or unconsciously those beliefs which were convenient to themselves.

Clearly then the postulate that God exists is not enough to make theology a science; we need to have also some postulate about his nature—otherwise we can believe about him what we choose and what will affect our conduct as we choose. It is as if we agreed that numbers exist, but resolved that two and

The Logic of God

two should be five or three as suited our convenience, and as if we imposed the three or the five theory by main force. Such a process, if it produced a uniformity of belief, would not be science, it would be merely war and would illustrate no law except that of the strongest.

But slowly, and even yet imperfectly, men have attained to the postulate that God, if he exists, must be good, entirely good : further that he must be good according to man's idea of goodness ; for if he were not, he would not be good at all according to any meaning we attach to the word. The progress to this postulate has been slow because, when first men said that God must be good, they still thought that he might have an idea of goodness different from man's, and so beliefs about God were not tested by man's idea of goodness. For instance, the Calvinist theory of predestination implied a standard for God quite different from ours ; he was forced to his beliefs about God by a logic which really sacrificed the idea of God's goodness to a dialectical process ; given certain other postulates about God, then he must behave in a devilish manner. The idea of God's goodness was really sacrificed to the postulates and the conclusions drawn from them, and men were told that God was good but not according to human ideas. The

55

result was that human ideas of goodness were themselves perverted by this forced notion of the goodness of God. But at last the human idea of goodness prevailed over the forced notion, and Calvinism is almost extinct because it assumes a God who is not good according to human ideas. Its logic has been broken by the imperious human demand that God shall be good according to human ideas; and also by the human demand for a conception of God that shall be useful and not mischievous. Theology is always in the long run, like any other science, tested by its practical application. And if it is to be a science it must be more and more so tested. It must be of use or it will cease to exist.

I must, however, digress for a moment in order to emphasize the distinction between the two kinds of logic—Formal Logic, and what I will call the Logic of growth. Formal Logic is that which unpacks. It tells you what is implied by a statement. It merely makes the result of one or two statements clear to you; it brings out what is already contained in them. Its characteristic expression is the syllogism. As a mental discipline this is useful enough. It forces you to obey the laws of your thought, to work out deductions from the postulates that have happened to your mind. It exposes contradiction and

The Logic of God

compels you to reject it. But in the last resort it is purely mechanical.

The other Logic, the Logic of growth, is concerned not with statements about facts, but with the facts themselves. Formal Logic implies a static world of statements always remaining the same. The other Logic assumes a self that is growing, and a world of other facts also growing; it looks away from propositions and has regard to reality. Thus, to take this particular case of the logic of God which is the supreme example of the logic of growth. There is the proposition that God is not merely good, but all we can imagine of goodness. You cannot make a syllogism of it, because the concept of goodness is one that cannot be unpacked. It is growing in you and all men ; further it is a universal concept shared by all men and contributed to by all out of their own common and growing experience. It has change in it, but the change of growth, not of external compulsion. So there is change in the idea of God as goodness. But if you say that God is goodness, you imply a belief that goodness itself is real and in its essence unchanging, not a quality of an opportunist character or one to be defined in terms of something else, such as the struggle for life. Goodness is a fact outside us, which we call God ; but we know this fact and its nature by our own growing conception of goodness. Thus we check our idea of God by that conception ; but on the other hand, we also check our conception of the nature of goodness by our idea of God. He makes the fact of goodness a real and final fact. He influences all our thought about it. So we reach the double conception of God as to be thought of according to our values, but as also being the source and criterion of those values.

But the progress to the postulate of God's essential goodness has been slow, because man's ideas of goodness are not certain or changeless. The good God of some is not the good God of another. There are still, for instance, those who think it is a part of the goodness of God to be angry and to punish, still those who expect him to interfere in human affairs, to demand sacrifice and expiation because it seems a part of human goodness to do these things. Of course, it is sometimes argued, human ideas of goodness may be purely opportunist or empirical ; they may be those ideas which help us most in the struggle for life ; our morality may be a product of the herd. If so, of course God and the function of God is still merely to act as an authority, useful for survival purposes, to impose herd morality until we no longer need such an authority and can do what is useful

The Logic of God

for survival purposes without being told that it is the will of God, or that we are attaining to his nature.

In that case the postulate alike of God and his goodness will fade from the mind of man, will no longer happen to it. But many now who do not believe in God refuse to accept the idea of a purely opportunist morality; indeed it is itself losing ground with our experience and with our growing sense that to accept it would make life intolerable and inexplicable more than ever. We have a growing belief in our " values," as being not opportunist or liable to complete change and at the mercy of circumstances, but as rather being a part of our reality and the reality of the universe. Values grow rather than change, they elucidate themselves with belief in them, the more we become conscious of them the more we trust in them. They are for us not products but producers, not made by our experience but makers of it. We have to discover them, but they are there to be discovered by acting on them; we do not make them nor does Nature; they make us.

So the postulate to which theology has attained, or is attaining, is this—That God, if he is at all, is according to our values; and the postulate that God is according to our values comes before the postulate that he is.

It is by means of the first belief that we shall attain to the second, if at all.

It follows that if theology is to be a science it must begin with the postulate that God, if he is, is according to our values. By means of them we shall attain to a knowledge of his nature, and as our values become clearer and stronger so we shall know more and more about God. In fact the logic of theology is the logic of values, not a logic based first of all upon any ascertained or assumed fact about God such as his omnipotence or his omniscience. If any theory we have of his omnipotence or omniscience conflicts with our values, gives us a God whom we cannot value, then we must sacrifice the theory to the value. The first postulate about God is that he is the supreme object of value, if he is at all. And if we cannot reconcile any possible God with our values, then there is no God. We will sacrifice all alleged existing Gods to the postulated though non-existent God we value ; as Butler says, we will give up Christ for Christ's sake.

By this means we shall make of theology a science with a logic of its own based upon a clear postulate ; and further we shall be able to apply it like other sciences to our conduct, as I hope shortly to show.

We must, however, examine certain objections to our postulate that God, if he exists, is good. For by good we imply human notions of goodness. The word means what *we* call good ; it cannot be taken to mean some other kind of goodness which to us would be bad.

It may be, and often has been said by those who believe in God, that his notion of goodness transcends ours ; but this saying, if it has any meaning, implies that our notions are imperfect, not utterly wrong. They are clearly imperfect in that they differ and change ; but, if they are utterly wrong, then we have no right to the word at all and it means nothing to us. It might mean something if we had all the same notion of goodness which was utterly wrong ; but since we have different notions and know it, we imply by the use of the word that there *is* a goodness independent of our notions of it, and that those notions are themselves good or bad in so far as they approach to or depart from the real goodness. No one really denies this ; for by goodness is meant not merely moral goodness, but a good of which moral goodness is only a part. Logically those to whom moral goodness is relative or opportunist should hold truth to be relative or opportunist. Yet for them truth does not depend upon our notions at all, truth is good and error bad, and we have to conform our notions to truth. That is the aim of all science and philosophy ;

and so it is the aim of all life to conform to a real goodness, and to discover it in all its different provinces. And all criticism of our ideas of goodness implies this real goodness, and implies that our ideas are aiming at it.

So we may take it as an axiom that God is good according to our ideas of goodness, and that any God who is not good according to those ideas is not God. But since our ideas are imperfect we cannot say finally that God is of this or that nature, only that, *if* he is, he is good, and that we have to discover his nature by the improvement in our own ideas of goodness.

But will this axiom be of any practical use or value? Clearly it will be, and already has been, of great use in criticizing ideas of God which make him out to be not good and so affect the conduct of men disastrously. Believe in a God who is not good, and you will not be good yourself. That is admitted by atheists; indeed it is one of their chief reasons for preaching atheism : *Tantum religio potuit suadere malorum.* Even the atheist would admit that men would be better if they believed in a good God than in a bad one. They sacrificed their children to Moloch ; they would not sacrifice their children to Christ, but rather themselves to their children. Still, if God is not, the belief in a good God rather

The Logic of God

than a bad one is a *pis aller*. The best is not to believe in a God at all, the truth being that there is no God. And it is the faith even of atheists, and particularly of them, that it is good to believe in truth at all costs, and that to believe a lie because it will make you good is to do evil that good may come. The good does not come thus. How then can the axiom that God is good—if he is good at all—affect conduct? How can it be applied to life?

It may be applied to destroy the belief in God. For men may find the facts of life incompatible with the existence of a good God, as many have done, and may give up the God rather than their ideas of goodness. In that case theology will be a means of destroying its very subject matter. It will prove to us that its axiom disproves its subject matter's existence. In which case it will at least be science and entitled to the respect of the most inveterate atheist. It will be like a despot who uses his power to establish a republic. Still theology, if a science, must take that risk, must not even think it a risk, since its aim is to discover the truth about God —whatever that truth may be. The only danger it must fear is falsehood, or else it is not a science. For, by definition, the one evil to a science is falsehood, the one good is truth.

The truth, then, with which theology starts,

the axiom which no one will deny, is that, if God is, he is good. Is that a barren axiom, or one on which any advance can be made ?

To begin with, it is an axiom which men have reached through tears and blood, not so much by reasoning as by the discovery of the long unknown desire of their hearts. Gods to begin with were not by definition good, nor was it the desire to believe in a good God that made men worship their gods. Rather they do not seem to have believed in the possibility of a good God. He was too good to be true. There were no doubt many reasons for the belief in God, some of which we do not know because we do not know enough of our own minds or the minds of primitive men. But the two chief reasons seem to have been the desire for an explanation of things and the desire for an authority.

The desire for an explanation is not what we should call scientific but rather practical. They associated explanation with use. If they could find the reason why things happen they would be able to make things happen as they would wish. This reason was to them, of course, personal, they had not reached the idea of a process ; and they believed that, if they could find the person, they might induce him to do what they wished, by magic or what not. So the desire to find this person

64

The Logic of God

led them to believe they had found him, and also to believe in the magic by which he could be influenced. In this desire there was no inkling of the dreadful effects of believing in what is false for practical purposes. For the whole process of belief was unconscious. But the result was that, since the God did not do what was wished, since the nature of things seemed to be often malign or at least capricious, the God who was the cause of all this nature seemed also to be malign or capricious, and must be placated by means contrary to the natural values of man, contrary, too, to all his real interests. Hence the horrors of primitive religion—in which also all the fears and hatreds of men for each other were expressed.

But besides an explanation, men have needed an authority for what they wished to do or believe, for what seemed to them most important in action or opinion. They were not content with their own opinions, about which there might be differences. The Jews, for instance, found that certain sanitary rules were of great value and they needed an authority for these rules outside themselves. They found it in Jehovah. Whatever was most necessary for them to do, he told them to do. That was part of his function. But they also needed his authority for their opinion of themselves and their enemies. They were

65

his chosen people, and those whom they hated
he hated. What they wished to do to their
enemies, he wished them to do. He was the
God of their national collective desire; he
justified it and made it part of the nature of
the universe turned into a law. So Jehovah
was for them a law-giver; and since they were
a people with a strong belief in law, but without
much passion for science, he became more and
more a lawgiver and a law-enforcer—with
hideous results for their defeated enemies.

Neither God the explanation, nor God the
authority, is necessarily good or likely to be
good. God the explanation has in him what
seems the malice or caprice of nature. God
the authority has in him all human exasperation against the disobedient or the hostile,
all pack instincts in fact; he is the gramophone
of the majority, like a daily paper, except that
he is more conservative. Both Gods still
survive in our theology and in our religion,
and we seek texts from the New Testament
and even the Old to justify what we wish to
do. But the explanation and the authority
Gods are not God, but non-existent beings
who bear the name of God. True there are
still those who believe that God is an explanation of the origin of things; but a moment's
thought will show that he is no more an explanation than the mechanical theory of the

66

The Logic of God

universe. As some one has said : The great question is, how did there ever come to be anything at all ? And that question applies to God as well as to matter, energy, life. It is no explanation to say that these things have gone on for ever or that God has gone on for ever. And if we say that God exists in eternity, not in time, that is only our way of saying we know nothing about it. We mean that the truth about him cannot be a truth that we are capable of conceiving. (But this statement has at least the advantage that it assumes a truth we are incapable of conceiving. The weakness of the mechanical theory is that it professes to state an ultimate truth we are capable of conceiving and then alleges something inconceivable about it, namely that it has gone on and will go on for ever.)

Religion in its beginning has often little connexion or no connexion with morality. The explanation God has none at all. But the Jewish authority God very early had some connexion with morality, because the Jews were a people with a strong sense of morality with which they invested their authority God. The connexion once established grew closer, though often the authority God impeded the advance of morality, since he gave his authority to a morality that otherwise might have been more quickly outgrown. He was often the means of preserving the pack morality from the criticism of individuals. Jehovah said this was right, and it must be right whatever Amos or Isaiah might say. But still, as morality was associated with the authority God, Amos and Isaiah also expressed their moral sense through his mouth. " Thus saith the Lord " was their way of expressing their values. They had the notion of a God revealed gradually and to each man through his own values, a God who was the God of the righteous, of the mystic, the artist, the saint, and not merely of the pack. So for them the idea of God loses its rigidity, he is the God of the present as well as the past. He is not merely the commander but also the inspirer. He is not merely the God who tells you what to do, what the collective desire in you dictates. He begins to satisfy the desire of your own heart and the idea of his goodness encroaches on the idea of his power. You can see the change when in the Old Testament certain writers begin to speak of the goodness more than of the power of God. They desire a God who will not cause a conflict between his law and their own consciences. They begin to believe that in his will is our peace. The conflict between them is between their own values, which are the revelation or very voice

The Logic of God

of God, and the baser part of themselves ; and for this conflict they can foresee an issue.

So whereas the Hebrew God at first is entirely a power outside them, utterly transcendent, as we say, you find even in the Old Testament the beginning of the belief in an immanence of the divine within man, which is his values, answering to the divine outside him.

It was the great theological achievement of Christianity to assert this doctrine of immanence and transcendence, though it has often been in abeyance in Christian theology and is very implicitly denied by many accepted dogmas. The reason is clear. Priests with their unconscious professional interest do not like the doctrine. It tells you that you yourself can be aware of God, can know him, not because he does spectacular miracles about which the priests tell you, but by means of the divine in yourself, namely your own values. This conflict between the immanent idea of God and the purely transcendent idea persists to this day. There is a persistent half-unconscious effort to get rid of the inconvenient immanent God or to reduce him to a minimum. Christ himself, the immanent God in his purity, the word made flesh, is not entirely the word made flesh. He has become transcendent after his short and unhappy experience of immanence. The whole pressure of the church

7

was on his transcendence for centuries, and we have to recover his immanence if Christianity is to survive at all.

But my concern in this essay is not with Christian theology, but with theology. I speak of the history of theology only to show that it has not yet become a science, and why. It has always been tainted with the idea of the explanation and authority God, both of whom are purely transcendent and about both of whom we can know only by revelation.

Even those who do not believe in God must be interested in the sudden proclamations of God's goodness made from time to time in the Old Testament. He remains the authority God, but an authority for new thoughts about himself. He does not care for sacrifice. He expresses the disgust of the prophet for all the blood and steam of the bullocks and rams. He hates his priests ; he hates people who talk solemn old nonsense ; above all he hates pack morality and the baying of the herds. How to-day he would hate the dull cruelty, the national flattery of the press. To the Jewish prophet or poet it is natural to say that God hates all these, when it is the best in himself, the great insurgent universal that looks to the future, which hates them. He is already far on the way to the doctrine of immanence, though he does not consciously state it. For of course mere transcendence cannot be alleged of a God who is always telling you things, always angry with you and punishing you. The purely transcendent God, as the Greek philosophers saw, can have no dealings with men, and men can have no knowledge of him. Job also saw this, and his God is the unknown who derides men's pretence to know about him. But the Jews were not philosophic. They wanted a God entirely above men who would act as an authority, a practical God who would confirm their own laws and hatreds; and they did not mind how inconsistent he was with his own nature, provided he worked. Nor did the prophets who began to imply immanence see what they implied. They merely said that God was good, meaning good according to man's idea of goodness; and the goodness of God grew, according with man's idea. Proclamations about his nature were made as the prophet saw more and more clearly what was goodness. So, while in the Old Testament prophets say that God is righteous, etc., St. John suddenly says " God is love "; and this he says because Christ has told us things about God which express his own profound and new sense of goodness.

In the teaching of Christ there is, I believe, a clear statement of the doctrine of immanence, though it has been overlooked because, when he preaches it, he is supposed to mean that he himself is a transcendent God. The notion that when Christ was proclaiming the doctrine of immanence he was proclaiming his own transcendent Godhead has affected the language of the Authorized Version and colours all our thought about him, even when we are not Christians. It has also coloured the evangelists' version of his words. But the doctrine of immanence to him was much more than a doctrine; an actual experience is always beating in his thought, trying to express itself. Of some things in the nature of God he is utterly sure because he is sure of their value in himself. And because they are beyond him, because they possess him, he knows they are God in him. He feels inspired like a musician or a poet. This is Nietzsche's account of his own experience:

"If one had the smallest vestige of superstition left in one, it would hardly be possible completely to set aside the idea that one is the mere incarnation, mouthpiece, or medium of an almighty power. The idea of revelation in the sense that something which profoundly convulses and upsets one becomes suddenly visible and audible with indescribable certainty and accuracy describes the simple fact. One hears—one does not seek; one takes—one does not ask who gives: a thought suddenly flashes up like lightning, it comes with necessity, without faltering. I have never had any choice in the matter."

It is true that with this sense of being possessed men do naturally turn to the transcendent that possesses them. They assume its independent reality. What they supremely value in themselves is not merely themselves. It makes them aware of a fellowship both with other men who share the same values and to whom they can communicate those values, and also with a source of all these values. And this sense of the source is stronger for them than all dialectic. Tell them that a perfectly good God is incompatible with the existence of evil, and they will smile at your argument. The perfectly good God may be incompatible with our reasoning about evil, but so much the worse for our reasoning. They begin with the God they know; and they will not deny their knowledge of him for any dialectical process. Who would, except a specialist in dialectic? If God appeared to me and convinced me by his own power that he was God, should I listen to any argument, no matter how skilful, which maintained that I could know nothing about external reality? I may be able to convince myself by argument that I know nothing about the reality of a tree when I am not experiencing a tree with any fullness, when I can put it to myself that I am aware of a tree only with my senses and that my senses are merely me. But when I am aware of a tree with my values also; when it becomes beautiful to me and part of a divine nature expressive of the universal beauty in all its growth and form and colour—then I pay no heed to his dialectic. My values, the deepest part of myself, cry out against it, or rather swamp it. A man in love does not doubt either the existence of the beloved or that he knows her; and the most precise dialectician, if he could fall in love, would then surrender his dialectic to his knowledge. He may prefer his game to passionate experience; but if so, he should know that it is a game, and that he is arguing about knowledge without experience of it. He is a half man legislating for whole men and telling them about themselves out of his ignorance.

The mystic is not, as many suppose, a teller of fairy tales about himself. He is one who prefers the richness of his own experience to diagrams of reality. He is concerned with what actually happens to him, not with what he knows by hearsay and then argues about. He may not go far into argument, but that is because he is busy experiencing. His sayings are about the full rich reality, and he will not think away from it. He is like an

artist for whom the visible world exists—
like Schubert, whose mind swarms with
melodies so that he does not wish or need to
develop them according to some system. You
may, if you like, say that others have more
mastery of form, but whom would you rather
listen to ?

So while you may believe, if you will, that
theologians or logicians have a sounder process,
you listen to Christ when he utters his doctrine
of immanence. You know by the very order
and sound of his words that he is telling of
what has happened to him. He is the inspired
man of science rather than the investigator.
Bacon's method of induction is not for him,
but he makes the discoveries—even if he cannot prove them.

This immediate sense of God without,
answering to God within, is not pragmatism.
Prophets and Mystics do not believe in the
immanent and transcendent God because he
works, but because they know him ; and they
do not ask us to believe in him because he
works but because, they say, if we will we may
know him also. There is in us also the immanent God if we will acknowledge him.

" For what man knoweth the things of a man,
save the spirit of man which is in him ? Even
so the things of God knoweth no man, but the
Spirit of God.

"Now we have received, not the spirit of the world, but the spirit which is of God, that we might know the things that are freely given to us of God." (1 Cor. ii. 11, 12.)

Upon this knowledge all the logic of God is based ; for logic must be based on some knowledge. But some logic increases knowledge, other does not, but merely says at the end what was implied at the beginning, and so persuades us that we advance, when we merely mark time. All men are mortal ; Socrates is a man ; therefore Socrates is mortal. But, All men are mortal, means that A B C and Socrates are mortal, and at the end I say that again. The other logic says God is God, all that there can be of Good ; and this is a growing logic, because I do not yet know what all there can be of Good is. To know that God is that, helps me to know more of what good is, just as to know what Good is, helps me to know what God is. The two statements act on each other, fertilize each other, like a man and woman in love. They are like the doctrine of faith and works, which also has a living and growing logic in it. The more you believe either doctrine, the more you know about both its terms. But the doctrine of mere transcendence or mere immanence is barren. Transcendence cuts off God from man, immanence cuts off man from God. Or, to leave

theology out of it, it cuts off goodness from
man, or man from goodness. It makes goodness static, achieved or impossible. The doctrine of transcendence means that my idea of
goodness is not mine but imposed on me by
an unintelligible God; and I have to obey it
without feeling it, without making it my
own. Or, in modern atheistical terms, it is
imposed on me by Nature, which is transcendent. I may call it goodness, but Nature,
if she could think or feel, would not call it
goodness. It would be merely an illusion she
imposes on me for her own purposes, if she
has purposes. It is not real, any more than
goodness is real for those who believe it to
be the will of a transcendent God. For them
it is not goodness, but the will of that God, just
as for the naturalist our goodness is not goodness but the will of Nature.

And so with immanence taken alone, my
idea of goodness is merely mine; again it has
no validity except for me; and because it is
mine and mine alone it is completely mine
and already perfect. I cannot logically hold
any doctrine of fellowship, any belief in
man's common achievement of a greater goodness; for how can there be a greater goodness,
if it is all in man already? What is the model
of men, but man, and how can they surpass
their model, if it is all? Either I fall back

utterly on myself—and how can I satisfy myself with myself?—or else I believe in the pack goodness, which again is achieved by the pack and can be improved only by more perfect uniformity, but without a model to be uniform with. A goodness merely immanent —the goodness of myself, the goodness of the pack—I cannot believe in. On the other hand a goodness utterly transcendent, and not mine at all, I cannot believe in. Both these kinds of goodness are achieved, barren, static ; and so they are not goodness at all. For goodness in man means to us effort. It is the nature of perfection in itself to be always opening, like a flower to the sun, and it implies a sun to open to. It is the nature of goodness to be aware of another goodness not yet achieved, not even experienced. That is what we mean by transcendence. It is the unknown that we know, and if you say that is a contradiction, it expresses a contradiction in our experience. We are aware of a goodness we do not know, we hunger and thirst after it. The musician's tune, which is beauty, expresses his hunger and thirst for a beauty he has not seen or heard. The saint's conduct, which is righteousness, expresses his hunger and thirst for a righteousness he has not, which he says is that of God. These escape into infinity and eternity, their excellence is beyond itself, already, because it strains after a transcendent excellence and makes us, by its very quality of infinity, aware of that infinity. But believe in immanence or transcendence alone, and you are shut up within yourself and your own experience of yourself. Both are nightmare concepts begotten of man's feebleness and fear of experience; and in them is the logic that prevents growth, not the logic that grows.

IV

Pooled Self-Esteem ∽ ∽ ∽

I

I AM, I confess, astonished at the lack of curiosity which even psychologists, and they more than most men, discover about the most familiar, yet most surprising, facts of the human mind. They have their formulæ, as that the human mind is unconsciously always subject to the sexual instinct; and these formulæ, while they make psychology easier for those who accept them, utterly fail to explain the most familiar, yet most surprising, facts.

There is, for instance, self-esteem—egotism —we have no precise scientific name for it; if we go by our own experience, it seems to be far more powerful and constant than the sexual instinct, far more difficult to control, and far more troublesome. The sexual instinct gets much of its power from this egotism, or self-esteem, and would be manageable without it; but self-esteem is, for many of us, unmanageable. Often we suppress it, but still it is

Pooled Self-Esteem

our chief obstacle to happiness or any kind of excellence ; and, however strong or persistent it may be in us, we never value it. In others we dislike it intensely, and no less intensely in ourselves when we become aware of it ; and, if a man can lose it in a passion for something else, then we admire that self-surrender above all things. In spite of the psychologists, we know that the sexual instinct is not the tyrant or the chief source of those delusions to which we are all subject. It is because we are in love with ourselves, not because we are in love with other people, that we make such a mess of our lives.

Now, what we ask of psychology, if it is to be a true science, is that it shall help us to manage ourselves so that we may achieve our deepest, most permanent desires. Between us and those desires there is always this obstacle of self-esteem ; and if psychology will help us to get rid of that, then, indeed, we will take it seriously, more seriously than politics, or machinery, or drains, or any other science. For all of these, however necessary, are subsidiary to the management of the self ; and all would be a thousand times better managed by a race of beings who knew how to manage themselves. There is not a science, or an art, that is not hampered by the self-esteem of those who practise it ; for it blinds us both to truth and to beauty, and most of us are far more unconscious of its workings than we are of the workings of our sexual instinct. The Greeks were right when they said, " Know thyself " ; but we have not tried to follow their advice. The self, in spite of all our attempts to analyse it away in physical terms, remains unknown, uncontrolled, and seldom the object of scientific curiosity or observation.

In the past, the great masters of religion were well aware of self-esteem ; and our deepest and most practical psychology comes from them, though we do not call it psychology. For them the problem was to turn self-esteem into esteem for something else ; and to that all other human problems were subsidiary. By God they meant that in which man can utterly forget himself ; and they believed in God because the self can sometimes utterly forget and lose itself in something which cannot be seen or touched, but which does cause self-forgetfulness. They were sure that the self could not so forget itself except in something more real than itself. " With thy calling and shouting," says St. Augustine, " my deafness is broken ; with thy glittering and shining, my blindness is put to flight. At the scent of thee I draw in my breath and I pant for thee ; I have tasted and I hunger and thirst ; thou hast touched me and I am on fire for thy

82

peace." Augustine had, no doubt, an exorbitant self, which tormented him ; and he was far more aware of his self-esteem and its workings than most men are, even to-day. He was concerned with a real, psychological fact, and his *Confessions* are still interesting to us because of that concern. And the Sermon on the Mount itself is also practical and psychological, concerned with the satisfaction of the self in something else, so that we are still interested in it, however little we may obey it. But still, from this supreme object of self-control, we turn to other tasks and sciences, at best only subsidiary.

We might begin by asking, if once our curiosity were aroused—Why are we born with this exorbitant self ? It seems to have no biological purpose ; it does not help us in the struggle for life, any more than in the arts and sciences, or in conduct, to be always esteeming, admiring, and relishing the self. The products of our egotism, open or suppressed, are useless and unvalued ; the very word vanity expresses our opinion of them. But what a vast part of ourselves is just vanity —far vaster than the part that is instinct or appetite. The demands of appetites cease, for the time, with their satisfaction, but the demands of vanity never. Consider, for instance, how your whole opinion of any man is affected by the fact that he has wounded or flattered your vanity. If he does either unconsciously, the effect on your opinion of him, on your whole feeling toward him, is all the greater; for your vanity knows that unconscious homage or contempt is the most sincere.

The greatest villain in literature, Iago, acts from vanity. He did not know it; we may not know it as we read the play; but Shakespeare knew it by instinct; he saw the possibilities of his own vanity in that of Iago, saw that it was cruel as the grave, and developed it in his tragedy of vanity. Those satanic criminals who seduce and murder woman after woman are not sex-maniacs, but vanity-maniacs, and their conquests feed their vanity more than their lust. They are imprisoned in the self, enslaved to it. And the great masters of religion, intensely aware of this tyrannical self in themselves, fear to be enslaved to it and cry to God for freedom. That is why they are almost morbidly, as it seems to us, concerned with sin. Sin means to them this exorbitant self, this vanity that may draw a man into any monstrous and purposeless villainy. They *will* not allow the analysis of sin into other and more harmless things, or the analysis of righteousness into other things less lovely. For them there is one problem—to be free of the self and of vanity, to be aware of

84

that which glitters and shines, which shouts
and calls to the self to forget itself and be at
peace. Sin is the blindness, deafness, captivity
of the self when it is turned in upon the self;
righteousness is its peace and happiness when
it is aware of that superior reality they call
God.

You may think them wrong in theory, but
in practice they are right; they are concerned
with the real human difficulty, and aiming at
that which all human beings do most deeply
and constantly desire. The riddle of life is
this riddle of the exorbitant self, which somehow or other must be satisfied, but can be
satisfied only when it forgets itself in a superior
reality. I say *satisfied*, because suppression or
self-sacrifice, as it is commonly understood, is
no solution of the problem. You can almost
kill the self by lack of interest; but if you do
that, you will not satisfy it and, in some
indirect way, its egotism will still persist and
work mischief in you.

Ascetics are often the worst egotists of all,
thinking about nothing but their own souls,
which means their own selves, living a life
of inner conquest and adventure, which is all
artificial because internal. Their interest,
because they refuse it to external reality, is
the more intensely concentrated on themselves;
their very God, to whom they incessantly

pray, is but an idol made and set up within the temple of the self and has no likeness to the real God, if there be one. Or it is like a medium, or the leading articles of a newspaper, telling them what they wish to be told, and persuading them that it is true because it seems to come from outside, whereas all the time it is really only the voice of the self echoed back. By those methods we can attain to no freedom because we attain to no self-knowledge or control or satisfaction.

If one is concerned purely with psychology, freed from all biological or other assumptions, one may conjecture that the self comes into life with all kinds of capacities or faculties itching to be exercised, and that the problem of life, for some reason a very hard one, is to find a scope for their exercise. We are born with all these faculties and capacities, but we are not born with a technique that will enable us to exercise them. And, if we never acquire it, then the self remains exorbitant, because they all, as it were, fester and seethe within it. It is as exorbitant as when we have an abscess at the root of a tooth and can think of nothing else. Any thwarting of a faculty, capacity, or appetite produces this exorbitance and tyranny of the self; but, since the satisfaction of faculties and capacities is, for most people, much harder than the satisfaction of appetites, the exorbitance of the self is more often caused by the thwarting of the former than of the latter. The problem of the satisfaction of appetites is comparatively simple, for it does not even need a technique of the mind. We can eat without learning to eat; we can make love, even, without learning to make love; but when it comes to turning the mind outward and away from itself, then it is the mind itself that has to learn, has to realize and discover its external interests by means of a technique painfully acquired.

Civilization means the acquirement of all the techniques needed for the full exercise of faculties and capacities, and, thereby, the release of the self from its own tyranny. Where men are vainest, there they are least civilized; and no amount of mechanical efficiency or complication will deliver them from the suppression of faculties and the tyranny of the self, or will give them civilization. But at present we are not aware how we are kept back in barbarism by the suppression of our faculties and the tyranny of our exorbitant selves. We shall discover that clearly and fully only when psychology becomes really psychology; when it concerns itself with the practical problems which most need solving; when it no longer tries to satisfy us with dogmas and formulæ taken from other sciences.

Essays on Religion

II

And now I come to the practical part of this article. I, like every one else, am aware that we are kept back in barbarism and cheated of civilization by war; but behind war there is something in the mind of man that consents to war, in spite of the fact that both conscience and self-interest are against it; and it seems to me that a real, a practical science of psychology would concern itself with this something, just as the science of medicine concerns itself with pestilence. And a real, a practical science of psychology would not be content to talk about the herd instinct, which is not a psychological but a biological hypothesis, and only a hypothesis. It would not say, " Man is a herd animal; therefore it is natural for herds of men to fight each other." In the first place, it would remember that herds of animals do not necessarily fight other herds; in the second, that we do not know that man, in his remote animal past, was a herd animal; and, in the third place, that, as psychology, it is concerned with the mind of man as it is, not with what other sciences may conjecture about the past history of man.

Now, if psychology asks itself what it is in the present mind of man, of the peoples we call civilized, that consents to war, it will at once have its attention drawn to the fact that

Pooled Self-Esteem

wars occur between nations, and that men have a curious habit of thinking of nations apart from the individuals who compose them ; and of believing all good of their own nation and all evil of any other which may, at the moment, be opposed to it. This is common-place, of course ; but, having stated the com-monplace, I wish to discover the reason of it. And I cannot content myself with the formula that man is a herd animal, not only because it is not proved, but also because there is no promise of a remedy in it. There is something in me, in all men, which rebels against this blind belief that all is good in my nation, and evil in some other ; and what I desire is some-thing to confirm and strengthen this rebellion. When we can explain the baser, sillier part of ourselves, then it begins to lose its power over us ; but the hypothesis of the herd instinct is not an explanation—it says, merely, that we are fools in the very nature of things, which is not helpful or altogether true. We are fools, no doubt, but we wish not to be fools ; it is possible for us to perceive our folly, to discern the causes of it, and by that very discernment to detach ourselves from it, to make it no longer a part of our minds, but something from which they have suffered and begin to recover. Then it is as if we had stimulated our own mental phagocytes against

bacilli that have infected the mind from outside; we no longer submit ourselves to the
disease as if it were health; but, knowing it
to be disease, we begin to recover from it.

The habit of believing all good of our own
nation and all evil of another is a kind of
national egotism, having all the symptoms and
absurdities and dangers of personal egotism,
or self-esteem; yet it does not seem to us to
be egotism, because the object of our esteem
appears to be, not ourselves, but the nation.
Most of us have no conviction of sin about it,
such as we have about our own egotism; nor
does boasting of our country seem to us vulgar,
like boasting of ourselves. Yet we do boast
about it because it is our country, and we
feel a warm conviction of its virtues which
we do not feel about the virtues of any other
country. But, when we boast and are warmed
by this conviction, we separate ourselves from
the idea of the country, so that our boasting
and warmth may not seem to us egotistical;
we persuade ourselves that our feeling for our
country is noble and disinterested, although
the peculiar delight we take in admiring it
could not be if it were not our country. Thus
we get the best of both worlds, the pleasures
of egotism without any sense of its vulgarity,
the mental intoxication without the mental
headaches.

Pooled Self-Esteem

But I will give an example of the process which, I hope, will convince better than any description of it. Most Englishmen, and, no doubt, most Americans, would sooner die than boast of their own goods. Yet, if some one says—some Englishman in an English newspaper—that the English are a handsome race, unlike the Germans, who are plain, an Englishman, reading it, will say to himself, " That is true," and will be gratified by his conviction that it is true. He will not rush into the street uttering the syllogism : " The English are a handsome race ; I am an Englishman ; therefore I am handsome ; " but, unconsciously and unexpressed, the syllogism will complete itself in his mind ; and, though he says nothing of his good looks even to himself, he will *feel* handsomer. Then, if he sees a plain German, he will say to himself, or will feel without saying it, " That poor German belongs to a plain race, whereas I belong to a handsome one." Americans may be different, but I doubt it.

So, if we read the accounts of our great feats of arms in the past, we ourselves feel braver and more victorious. We teach children in our schools about these feats, and that they are characteristic of Englishmen, or Americans, or Portuguese, as the case may be ; and we never warn them, because we never warn ourselves, that there is egotism in their pride and in their belief that such braveries are peculiarly characteristic of their own country. Yet every country feels the same pride and delight in its own peculiar virtues and its own pre-eminence; and it is not possible that every country should be superior to all others.

Further, we see the absurdity of the claims of any other country clearly enough, and the vulgarity of its boasting. Look at the comic papers of another country and their patriotic cartoons; as Americans, look at *Punch* and especially at the cartoons in which it expresses its sense of the peculiar virtues, the sturdy wisdom, the bluff honesty, of John Bull, or the lofty aims and ideal beauty of Britannia; or those other, less frequent, cartoons, in which it criticizes or patronizes the behaviour of Jonathan and the ideals of Columbia. Does it not seem to you incredible, as Americans, that any Englishmen should be so stupid as to be tickled by such gross flattery, or so ignorant as to be deceived by such glaring misrepresentations? Have you never itched to write something sarcastic to the editor of *Punch*, something that would convince even him that he was talking nonsense? Well, Englishmen have just the same feelings about the cartoons in American papers; and just the same blindness about their own. Disraeli

Pooled Self-Esteem

said that every one likes flattery, but with royalty you lay it on with a trowel; and nations are like royalty, only more so: they will swallow anything about themselves while wondering at the credulity of other nations.

What is the cause of this blindness? You and I, as individuals, have learned at least to conceal our self-esteem;. we are made uneasy by gross flattery; we are like the Duke of Wellington, who, when grossly flattered by Samuel Warren, said to him: "I am glad there is nobody here to hear you say that."

"Why, your Grace?" asked Warren.

"Because," answered the duke, "they might think I was damned fool enough to believe you."

But when our country is flattered, and by one of our countrymen, we do not feel this uneasiness; at least, such flattery is a matter of course in the newspapers and at public meetings in all countries; there is such a large and constant supply of it that there must be an equally large and constant demand. Yet no one can doubt that it is absurd and dangerous, if not in his own country, in others. Believe, if you will, that all the praises of your own country are deserved, and all the more, because of that belief, you will see that the praises of other countries are not deserved. If America is superior to all other countries in all essential virtues, then, clearly, all the other countries cannot be superior, and there must be some cause for their blind belief in their superiority. Englishmen, for instance, however bad their manners, do not proclaim, or even believe, that they are individually superior to all other men—indeed, you hold that the bad manners of Englishmen come from their belief, not in their individual superiority, but in the superiority of England; if they could be rid of that, they might be almost as well-mannered as yourselves. It is a national vanity, a national blindness, that makes fools of them.

But what is the cause of a folly so empty of either moral, or æsthetic, or even biological value, so dangerous indeed, not only to the rest of the world, but even to themselves? For the danger of this folly, its biological uselessness, has been proved to us in the most signal and fearful manner lately by the Germans. They cultivated national vanity until it became madness; and we are all aware of the results. But, if we suppose that they behaved so because they were Germans and therefore born mad or wicked, we shall learn nothing from their disaster. They were, like ourselves, human beings. There, but for the grace of God, goes England, goes America even; and whence comes this madness from

Pooled Self-Esteem

which the grace of God may not always save us? Because it exists everywhere, and is not only tolerated but encouraged, it must satisfy some need of the mind, however dangerously and perversely. Where there is a great demand for dangerous drugs, it is not enough to talk indignantly of the drug-habit. That habit is but a symptom of some deeper evil, something wrong with the lives of the drug-takers, for which the drug is their mistaken remedy; and the right remedy must be found if the habit is to be extirpated.

National egotism, I believe, is a kind of mental drug, which we take because of some unsatisfied need of our minds; and we shall not cure ourselves of it until we discover what causes our craving for national flattery and also our dislike and contempt of other countries. Somewhere, as in the case of all drug-taking, there is suppression of some kind; and the suppression, I suggest, is of individual egotism. We are trained by the manners and conventions of what we call our civilization to suppress our egotism; good manners consist, for the most part, in the suppression of it. However much we should like to talk of ourselves, our own achievements and deserts, we do not wish to hear others talking about theirs. The open egotist is shunned as a bore by all of us; and only the man, who for some reason is unable to suppress his egotism, remains an open egotist and a bore, persists in the I—I—I of childhood, and provokes the impatience caused by the persistence of all childish habits in the grown-up.

But this suppression of egotism is not necessarily the destruction of it, any more than the suppression of the sexual instinct is the destruction of that. And, in fact, our modern society is full of people whose egotism is all the more exorbitant and unconsciously troublesome to themselves because it is suppressed. Their hunger for praise is starved, but not removed; for they dare not even praise themselves. Ask yourself, for instance, whether you have ever been praised as much as you would like to be? Are you not aware of a profound desert in yourself which no one, even in your own family, has ever fully recognized? True, you have your faults, but, unlike the faults of so many other people, they are the defects of your qualities. And then there is in you a sensitiveness, a delicacy of perception, a baffled creative faculty even, in fact, an unrealized genius, which might any day realize itself to the surprise of a stupid world. Of all this you never speak—and in that you are like every one else in the stupid world. For all mankind shares with you, dumbly, this sense of their own profound

desert and unexpressed genius—and if, by
some ring of Solomon or other talisman, we
were suddenly forced to speak out the truth,
we should all proclaim our genius without
listening to each other.

I, for my part, believe in it, believe that it
does exist, not only in myself, but in all men ;
and the men of acknowledged genius are those
who have found a technique for realizing it.
I say *realizing*, because, until it is expressed
in some kind of action, it does not fully exist ;
and the egos of most of us are exorbitant,
however much we may suppress their outward
manifestations, because they do not succeed
in getting themselves born. The word in us
is never made flesh ; we stammer and bluster
with it, we seethe and simmer within ; and,
though we may submit to a life of routine and
suppression, the submission is not of the whole
self : it is imposed on us by the struggle for
life and for business purposes : and, unknown
to ourselves, the exorbitant, because unexpressed, unsatisfied ego finds a vent somehow
and somewhere.

III

Self-esteem is the consolation we offer to
the self because it cannot, by full expression,
win esteem from others. Each one of us is to
the self like a fond mother to her least gifted

son : we make up to it for the indifference of the world ; but not consciously, for in conscious self-esteem there is no consolation. If I said to myself, " No one else esteems me ; therefore I will practise self-esteem "—the very statement would make the practice impossible. It must be done unconsciously and indirectly, if it is to be done at all and to give us any satisfaction. Most of us have now enough psychology to detect ourselves in the practice of self-esteem, unless it is very cunningly disguised : and, what is more, we are quick to detect each other. It is, indeed, a convention of our society, and a point of good manners, to conceal our self-esteem from others, and even from ourselves, by a number of instinctive devices. One of the chief of these is our humour, much of which consists of self-depreciation, expressed or implied ; and *we* delight in it in spite of the subtle warning of Doctor Johnson, who said, " Never believe a man when he runs himself down ; he only does it to show how much he has to spare."

By devices like these we persuade ourselves that we have got rid of the exorbitant ego, that we live in a happy, free, civilized, de-egotized world. We are not troubled by the contrast between our personal modesty and our national boasting, because we are not aware of the connexion between them. But

Pooled Self-Esteem

the connexion, I believe, exists ; the national boasting proves that we have not got rid of our self-esteem, but only pooled it, so that we may still enjoy and express it, if only in an indirect and not fully satisfying manner. The pooling is a *pis aller*, like the floating of a limited company when you have not enough capital to finance some enterprise of your own ; but it is the best we can do with an egotism that is only suppressed and disguised, not transmuted.

If I have an exorbitant opinion of myself, it is continually criticized and thwarted by external criticism ; I learn, therefore, not to express it, and even forget that I have it ; but all the while I am seeking, unconsciously, for some means by which I can give it satisfaction. It becomes impossible for me to believe that I am a wonder in the face of surrounding incredulity ; so I seek for something, seeming not to be myself, that I can believe to be a wonder, without arousing criticism or incredulity ; in fact, something which others also believe to be a wonder, because it seems to them not to be themselves.

There are many such things, but the largest, the most convincing, and the most generally believed in, is Our Country. A man may, to some extent, pool his self-esteem in his family ; but the moment he goes out into the world, he is subject to external criticism and incredulity. Or he may pool it in his town ; but, as I have heard, the Bostonian-born is subject to the criticism and incredulity of the inhabitants of other towns. What, therefore, we need, and what we get, is a something which at the same time distinguishes us from a great part of the human race, and yet is shared by nearly all those with whom we come in contact. That we find in our country ; and in our country we do most successfully and unconsciously pool our self-esteem. True, there are other countries also pooling their self-esteem in the same way, and apt to criticize us and to question our pre-eminence ; but they are far away and we can think of them as an absurd, degenerate horde or rabble ; we can look at their newspapers and cartoons in our own atmosphere, and laugh at them securely. They have, indeed, a useful function in the heightening of our own pooled self-esteem ; for we are able, from a distance, to compare ourselves, *en masse*, with them, and to feel how fortunate we are, with a kind of hereditary merit, to be born different from them—

> When Britain first, at Heaven's command,
> Arose from out the azure main—

then also it was the command of Heaven that we should in due course be born Britons, and share in the glory of the mariners of England who guard our native seas ; and there is not one of us who, crossing from Dover to Calais for the first time, does not feel that he is more at home on his native seas than any seasick Frenchman.

All this is amusing enough to Americans in an Englishman, or to Englishmen in an American ; but it is also very dangerous. In fact, it is the chief danger that threatens our civilization, that prevents it from being civilized, and so, secure. We are all aware of private vices, even of individual self-esteem and its dangers ; but this great common vice, this pooled self-esteem, we still consider a virtue and encourage it by all means in our power. And this we do because we are not aware of its true nature and causes. We think that it is disinterested, when it is only the starved ego consoling itself with a *pis aller* ; we suppose that it is necessary to the national existence, when the Germans have just proved to us that it may ruin a most prosperous nation. Still we confuse it with real patriotism, which is love of something not ourselves, of our own people and city and our native fields, and which, being love, does not in the least insist that that which is loved is superior to other things, or people, unloved because unknown. We know that where there is real affection

9

there is not this rivalry or enmity; no man, because he loves his wife, makes domestically patriotic songs about her, proclaiming that she is superior to all other wives; nor does he hate or despise the wives of other men. In true love there is no self-esteem, pooled or latent, but rather it increases the capacity for love; it makes the loving husband see the good in all women; and he would as soon boast of his own wife as a religious man would boast of his God.

So the true love of country may be clearly distinguished from the patriotism that is pooled self-esteem by many symptoms. For the patriotism that is pooled self-esteem, though it make a man boast of his country, does not make him love his countrymen. Germans, for instance, before the war, showed no great love of other Germans, however much they might sing " Deutschland über Alles "; and in England, the extreme Jingoes, or nationalists, are always reviling their countrymen for not making themselves enough of a nuisance to the rest of the world. To them the British Empire is an abstraction, something to be boasted about and intrigued for; but real, living Englishmen are, for the most part, unworthy of it. Their patriotism, because it is pooled self-esteem, manifests itself in hatred rather than in love; just because it cannot

Pooled Self-Esteem

declare itself for what it is, because it is suppressed and diverted, its symptoms are always negative rather than positive. For, being suppressed and diverted, it can never find full satisfaction like the positive passion of love. So it turns from one object of hate to another, and from one destructive aim to another. Germany was the enemy and Germany is vanquished ; another enemy must be found, another danger scented ; and there are always enough patriots in every country, suffering from pooled self-esteem, to hail each other as enemies, and to play the game of mutual provocation.

So no league of nations, no polite speeches of kings and presidents, prime ministers and ambassadors, will keep us from hating each other and feeling good when we do so, unless we can attain to enough self-knowledge to understand why it is that we hate each other, and to see that this mutual hate and boasting are but a suppressed and far more dangerous form of that vanity which we have learned, at least, not to betray in our personal relations. In fact, the only thing that can end war is psychology applied to its proper purpose of self-knowledge and self-control. If once it can convince us that, when we boast of our country, we are suffering from pooled self-esteem, then we shall think it as vulgar and dangerous to boast of our country as to boast of ourselves. And, further, we shall be ashamed of such boasting, as a symptom of failure in ourselves. For pooled self-esteem is self-esteem afraid to declare itself, and it exists because the self has not found a scope for the exercise of its own faculties.

Why did the Germans suffer so much from pooled self-esteem before the war ? Because they were a suppressed and thwarted people. The ordinary German was wounded in his personal self-esteem by all the social conventions of his country ; he was born and bred to a life of submission ; and, though consciously he consented to it, unconsciously his self-esteem sought a vent and found it in the belief that, being a German, he was in all things superior to those who were not Germans. The more submissive he was as a human being, the more arrogant he became as a German ; and, with unconscious cunning, his rulers reconciled him to a life of inferiority by encouraging him in his collective pride. So, even while he behaved as if he were the member of an inferior, almost conquered, race, to his military caste, he told himself that this was the price he gladly paid for national pre-eminence.

Before and during the war the Germans were always saying that they had found a

Pooled Self-Esteem

new way of freedom through discipline and obedience; unlike the vulgar, anarchical, democracies of the West, they stooped to conquer; and, since they did it willingly, it was freedom, not servitude. But their psychology was as primitive as it was dangerous. That willingness of theirs was but making the best of a bad job. If only they had known it, they were not content with their submission; no people so intelligent in some things, so industrious and so self-conscious, could be content. There was in them a dangerous, unsatisfied stock of self-esteem, which, since they dared not express it in their ordinary behaviour, found expression at last in a collective national madness. It seems to us now that the German people suffered from persecution mania; but that mania was the vent by which every German eased his sense of individual wrong and soothed his wounded personal pride. By a kind of substitution, he took revenge for the sins of his own Junkers upon all rival nations; and hence the outbreak which seemed to us incredible even while it was happening.

I speak of this now only because it is a lesson to all of us, Americans and English. We too are thwarted, not so systematically as the Germans, but still constantly, in our self-esteem; and we too are constantly tempted to console ourselves by pooling it. In all industrial societies, the vast majority never find a scope for the full exercise of their faculties, and are aware of their inferiority to the successful few. This inferiority may not be expressed politically or in social conventions ; in America, and even in England, the successful may have the wit not to insist in any open or offensive manner upon their success ; but, all the same, it gives them a power, freedom, and celebrity which others lack. And this difference is felt far more than in the past, because now the poor live more in cities and know better what the rich are doing. Unconsciously, they are wounded in their self-esteem by all that they read in the papers of the doings of the rich ; they have become spectators of an endless feast which they do not share, with the result that they pool their wounded self-esteem either in revolutionary exasperation or in national pride. But, since national pride seems far less dangerous to the rich and successful than revolutionary exasperation, with the profound, unconscious cunning of instinct they encourage national pride by all means in their power.

There, I think, they are wrong. I believe that national pride, and the hatred of other nations, is a more dangerous vent for pooled self-esteem even than revolutionary exasperation ; for, sooner or later, it will, as in Russia, produce a revolutionary exasperation all the more desperate because it has been deferred and deceived. If we have another world war —and we shall have one unless we discover and prevent the causes of war in our own minds—there will be revolutionary exasperation everywhere ; and it will be vain to tell starving mobs that it is all the fault of the enemy. The chauvinism of the disinherited mob is but a drug, which increases the evil it pretends to heal. Behind revolutionary exasperation, and behind chauvinism, there is the same evil at work, namely, the thwarting of faculties, the sense of inferiority, the disappointed ego ; and we must clearly understand the disease if we are to find the remedy.

The remedy, of course, is a society in which faculties will no longer be suppressed, in which men will cure themselves of their self-esteem, not by pooling it, but by caring for something not themselves more than for themselves. To dream of such a society is as easy as to accomplish it is difficult ; but we shall have taken the first step toward the accomplishment of it when we see clearly that we have no alternative except a relapse into barbarism. Suppression, good manners, discipline, will never rid us of our self-esteem ; still it will find a vent in some collective, and so more dangerous, form, unless we can, as the psychologists say, sublimate it into a passion for something not ourselves. If we believe that our country is not ourselves, we deceive ourselves ; we may give our lives for it, but it is still the idol in which we pool our self-esteem ; and the only way to escape from the worship of idols is to find the true God.

I am not now talking religion ; I am talking psychology, though I am forced to use religious terms. The true God is to be found by every man only through the discovery of his deepest, most permanent desires ; and these he can discover only through the exercise of his highest faculties. So that is the problem for all of us ; and, as we now know, it is a collective problem, one which we can solve only all together. So long as other men are thwarted in the exercise of their highest faculties, you are thwarted also ; you are kept always from happiness by the unhappiness of others.

You may be rich, brilliant, and a lover of peace ; but, so long as the mass of men can do nothing with their self-esteem but pool it, you will live in a world of wars and rumours of wars. You may be an artist, a philosopher, a man of science ; but, so long as the mass of men are set by division of labour to tasks in which they cannot satisfy the higher demands of the self, any demagogue may tempt them to destroy all that you value. Until they also enjoy and so value it, it is not secure for you or for the world.

In the past religion has failed because the problem of release from self-esteem has been for it a private and personal one. That is where psychology can now come to its aid. When once we understand that our self-esteem, if suppressed, is pooled, not destroyed, and that we can escape from it only by the exercise of our higher faculties, we shall see also that the problem of release is collective. We are, indeed, all members one of another, as the masters of religion have always said; but only now is it possible for us to see the full truth of their saying. In the past there often seemed to be some incompatibility between religion and civilization; but now we are learning that they are one, and have the same enemy. Once men sought for God alone, and in the wilderness; now we may be sure that they will not find Him unless they search all together. Salvation itself is not a private making of our peace with God : it is a common making of our peace with each other; and that we shall never do until, by self-knowledge, we remove the causes of war from our own minds.

All that I have said in this article is vague, loose, and amateurish; and I have fallen into religious language now and again because there was no other that I could use. But the science that we all need, if we are all together to be saved, does not yet exist. I have written to point out our bitter need of it, and in the hope that the demand will produce the supply.

V

Evil and the New Psychology ✑

I

THE new psychology appears to be making a discovery, the first promise of which is not yet perceived, even by the psychologists. This discovery is difficult to state, both because it is not yet fully made, and because it concerns the human mind, about which we know so little that we have not even words to express that little precisely. I will, therefore, ask the reader to forgive me if my statement fails to satisfy him.

It is being made in the effort to cure certain mental disorders, such as those which are called *phobias*. The phobia, it appears, has its origin in the mental history of the patient, in some shock or other mischance which he has forgotten. The fact that he has forgotten the origin is itself part of the cause of the phobia; and, if the origin can by some means be discovered and made known to the patient, then he will be able to cure himself of the phobia. The whole process, though seeming to work mechanically, is mental. It is like putting a machine in order, except that the machine knows that it is out of order and rights itself by becoming aware of the origin of its disorder. The healing knowledge comes from outside, from the psycho-analyst, yet it also comes as knowledge to the patient. It is absorbed mentally, just as medicine is absorbed physically; and then, like medicine, it works, the patient cannot tell how, but still mentally.

Now, as I have said, the full promise of this discovery is not commonly perceived, even by psychologists; for, in the first place, they have not yet insisted that it can be extended to the errors and moral perversities of normal people; and, in the second, they are often prevented by certain unconscious assumptions of their own from seeing what a new light it throws upon the whole problem of evil. These two points are closely connected with each other, so that the first will lead me naturally to the second. I will, then, begin with the first, namely, the extension of the discovery to the errors and perversities of normal people.

We are all aware, or should be, that our common method of dealing with each other's errors, namely, by controversy, is not successful; its failure is well expressed in the lines :

A man convinced against his will
Is of the same opinion still.

Evil and the New Psychology

That is to say, a man convinced against his
will is not convinced. Indeed, you cannot
convince him of any error, thoroughly established in his mind, by a rational process ; for
the error itself was not established by a
rational process. The psycho-analysts, when
they deal with a phobia, are aware of this.
They do not argue with a patient, do not
tell him that it is absurd to be afraid of
edged tools or of open spaces, or what not.
They know that argument in such cases is
like rubbing a sore : it only makes the
patient more aware of his disorder, and so
more convinced of its reality. The psycho-
analyst's method is, rather, to assume that it
is a mere disorder, to place it in the category
of disease, not in that of reason ; and to tell
the patient how it has come about. Then,
for the patient also, it passes out of the category
of reason into that of disease ; and, when he
knows the cause of it, it becomes to him something finite, mechanical, external, and so loses
its intimidating power over him. Instead of
classing it with madness, he classes it with
toothache ; and this very classification, by
separating it, as it were, from the whole
system of his mind, is itself a cure.

Thus it is that we should deal with error,
both in others and, finally, in ourselves. We
should, to begin with, understand that the

processes by which truth and error establish themselves in the mind are different; and, wherever we find error firmly established, we should seek for the cause of it and explain that cause to the person who is in error. Argument, in such cases, is worse than useless; for it treats error as if it were of the same nature as truth, takes it seriously, and assumes its origin to be rational. Further, when we attack a man's errors by argument, we enlist all his self-love in defence of them. They are to him part of himself; but, if he is to renounce them, he must be persuaded that they are not part of himself, but an accident that has happened to him, like a phobia.

Opinions or beliefs, once very firmly held, often vanish from our minds, without our knowing why or how they have vanished. We may think that some argument has destroyed them, and then wonder why we have seen the force of this argument at last, when we have been familiar with it so long without heeding it. In such cases the argument is usually a mere summons to surrender: the battle has really been fought, and the victory won, in the unconscious; for the cause of our belief has, for some reason, disappeared, and the belief itself has remained only until challenged. The cause of a false belief is really an obstacle to perception of the truth, and, that obstacle removed, the truth is seen. At present, this removal of obstacles is often a matter of chance; but the discovery of the new psychology should help us to effect it deliberately, in ourselves and in others. The mere knowledge that there may be causes of our dearest beliefs, unknown to ourselves, should set us examining those beliefs with a new and more critical curiosity; for there is not one of us that really wishes to believe nonsense. We believe it because some particular credulity in our minds makes it appear to be sense; and credulity is always particular, not general; it is a tendency to believe, not any nonsense, but some favourite kind of nonsense. For it has always a particular cause; and, when once that is discovered, the beliefs in which the credulity expresses itself do not need to be argued with : they have lost their prestige for us, like an often repeated tune the melody of which has turned to stale sentimentality. Yet, even when we have discovered the cause of a credulity, we seldom connect that discovery with the resulting change of belief. The change works in the unconscious, just as a patient is cured of a phobia without seeing how he is cured.

Suppose, for instance, that you believe more ill about some one than is true. That is because you have a readiness to believe ill about him—

a credulity on that point for which there is a cause, not a reason. The credulity means a resentment against him, which, like a phobia, has power over you just because you are not aware of its cause. But then, suppose you suddenly become aware, by some means, of the cause of this resentment—as that he has wounded your vanity, or has caused you some loss of income, or that for some reason you are afraid of him. This cause you have hidden from yourself because you wished to enjoy the resentment and could do so only by rationalizing it ; that is to say by believing that the man's actions and character justified it. But, the moment you are aware of the cause, the resentment itself loses its charm for you and is reduced to its proper proportions. Though, perhaps, the man has really behaved ill to you, your pleasure will no longer be in your anger, but rather in trying to be just in spite of it. You will judge yourself for your resentment, as well as him for provoking it. Your whole state of mind toward him will have lost its prestige and you will see it as having, not a reason, but a cause which it is your business to remove.

Resentments are just like phobias in this, that they are greatest and most dangerous to right thinking and feeling when the cause of them is unknown ; then the mind is poisoned by them, as the body by a festering, covered wound. So, if you find yourself thinking and feeling about some one altogether in terms of some resentment, you may be sure that it has an unknown cause. Find the cause, and you will isolate the resentment from the rest of your mind. You will see it in its danger and ugliness, and have the will to rid yourself of it. We all have within us a will to be sane, and it acts as soon as we become aware of the caused insanity of any of our beliefs, of the feelings which make us credulous ; for the beliefs are but a rationalizing of the feelings.

And this is true, not only of particular errors, such as we can detect in each other when we do not share them, but also of collective beliefs held by great masses of people, such as nations, or even by whole generations of every nation. The way to destroy these also is, not to argue with them, but to discover their cause and state it clearly. Only so can their prestige be destroyed.

If, for instance, it can be shown that a theological belief has been developed and maintained by a priesthood in its own professional interests, then it will lose its prestige for the laity, and even for the priesthood. Or if it can be shown that the whole doctrine of *laisser-faire* had its cause in the desire of people with capital to get every possible advantage

from their capital without doing violence to
their consciences, then that doctrine also will
lose its prestige, even for them. But in all
such cases the cause must be discovered and
stated with precision, so that it will be clear,
even to unwilling minds. Then it will gradually and unconsciously work its effect upon
them, and they will find themselves no longer
able to believe what they have believed, for
their own comfort. It is impossible for us to
believe anything for our comfort as soon as
we know that that is why we have been believing it. The process of comforting belief must
be unconscious. To make us conscious of it
is to end it.

Behind most, if not all, of our common and
persistent erroneous beliefs there is some kind
of fear; they are of the nature of phobias,
though the fear, being an *entirely* negative
and, therefore, unpleasant feeling, disguises
itself in some more positive form. And even
beliefs not altogether erroneous are constantly
tainted and perverted by an element of fear.
For instance, the belief in God and the belief
in immortality have, all through the ages,
been perverted by fear; in fact our minds are
infested with inherited and habitual phobias,
against which, hitherto, we have had no
defence, since we were not even aware of the
distinction between them and rational beliefs,

Evil and the New Psychology

or that in that distinction lay the promise of a cure. But now the promise has dawned upon us ; and it remains to apply a scientific cure to all error, to discover and state its causes with precision. For, without precision of statement, there can be no conviction ; but, with it, the conviction will come silently and irresistibly, since it will enlist the will to be sane, which is, in every man, on its side.

II

Unfortunately, the fulfilment of that promise is also hindered, as I have said, by certain unconscious assumptions of the psychologists, which make the promise itself seem a threat to the freedom of the mind. A great psychologist once said to me that he wished to free psychology altogether from philosophy. I answered that I did not know whether he could do it, or was right in trying to do it, but that he would certainly be right if he tried to free psychology from unconscious metaphysical assumptions. I was thinking of certain assumptions which seem to be often made by the Freudians, and which blind them to the promise of their great discovery. For they, finding the causes of evil in the mind, and by that means often removing the evil, make no distinction, in this matter, between right and wrong processes of the mind, but assume that

119

the right processes are caused in the same way as the wrong.

That is their theory, but not, of course, their practice. They are able to remove a phobia from the mind by discovering its cause, but they do not try to remove a true belief by discovering its cause; and, if they did, they would find it impossible, not merely because the discovery of the cause would fail to remove the belief, but also because the cause of true beliefs, and, indeed, of all right processes in the mind, cannot be discovered.

The Freudian might admit this in the case of true beliefs; but he will not admit it in the case of other right processes. For instance, having discovered that many mental disorders are caused by the sexual instinct working in the unconscious, he is apt to assume that all the normal processes of the mind are controlled by the sexual instinct. He will tell you that all art is a disguised expression of the sexual instinct, because many failures and perversities of art can so be explained. And there are psychologists who will tell you that all morals are a product of the gregarious instinct, because we can often detect that instinct in bad morals. The assumption in both cases is that, behind the self and more real than the self, are a number of impersonal, and indeed mechanical, forces called instincts, into which

Evil and the New Psychology

the self can be analysed away. As another psychologist once said to me : " Freud bombs the self into fragments and then hands the fragments back to you with a complacent smile."

We have a right to be suspicious of all theories that are incompatible with practice ; and no theory is more incompatible with the universal practice of mankind—and indeed of the Freudians—than this. For in practice, as I have said, they seek among these instincts only for the causes of what is wrong with the mind ; and they know when they have found these causes, because, by finding them, they are able to set the mind right. This test they cannot apply, even if they would, the other way. No one has ever yet destroyed a true belief by discovering its causes ; *for true beliefs have reasons, not causes.* Further, no one has yet discredited a right morality by connecting it with the gregarious instinct ; nor has anyone made good art seem bad, or deterred the artist from producing it, by asserting that it is an expression of the sexual instinct. We may find in the egotism of mankind a cause for the once universal belief that the earth was the centre of the universe ; we can find no cause for the belief that the sun is the centre of our solar system, except the fact that it is true.

We may see the working of the gregarious
instinct in much conventional morality; we
may even suddenly become aware of that
instinct in our own morality; but to see it
is to discredit the morality. We are not
aware of it in the morals of Socrates or of
Christ, which are to us morals and arouse our
sense of moral value because they revolt
against the tyranny of the gregarious instinct.
They are not caused as gregarious morality is
caused; at least there is no cause which we
can detect in them, which, when detected,
discredits them. As we accept a true belief
because it is true, so we accept their morals
because they are good.

Again, it is the bad or the half-insane artist
who finds a vent in his art for his unsatisfied
appetites; and a psychologist can explain the
causes of his failure so that we are convinced
by the explanation. But, if he tries to explain
success in art in the same way, we are not
convinced, nor is the artist. I may see unconscious, unsatisfied, sexual instinct in some
religious picture that revolts me with its
sensuality disguised as sentimentality; or the
discovery of that instinct may put me out of
conceit with a picture that I myself have liked
because it made a disguised appeal to my own
sexual instinct. But I cannot see sex at all
in Rembrandt's Supper at Emmaus, or in

Mozart's G minor quintet; nor would it put me out of conceit with these to be told that there was disguised sex in them. That would be merely theory to me, even if I believed it: it would have no practical effect on my feelings such as is produced by the discovery and precise statement of the causes of bad art. And the reason here, as in the other cases, is that good art has not causes, like bad art. I accept it because it is beautiful, as I accept a true belief because it is true, or good morals because they are good. Certainly, there is good art in which sex is the theme; but it is consciously chosen by the artist as his theme. It was not the sexual instinct that caused Correggio to paint his Antiope; nor is it the sexual instinct that causes us to admire it. The picture cannot be discredited by imputing a sexual cause to it; for whatever there is of sex in it is conscious, both in the artist and in the spectator, being theme and not cause.

In fact, the whole theory of the unconscious, advanced by Freud and confirmed with so many valuable practical results, implies just that difference between the right and wrong processes of the mind which the Freudians tend to deny. The sexual instinct, they say, is dangerous to us when it is disguised; and that must be true also of other instincts, such as the gregarious. And the reason is that these instincts can control the processes of the mind only when it is unaware of their control. It is then that they act as hidden causes, even of thought, mastering and perverting the three spiritual activities—the moral, the intellectual, and the æsthetic. But this tyranny can be ended, as phobias can be ended, by becoming aware of it ; and the Freudian method is to make us aware of it, and so to appeal to some other power in the mind which is stung into action as soon as it sees its enemies. Yet, according to the Freudian metaphysic, there is no other power. It is the instincts that become aware of themselves, not a self that becomes aware of them ; and the Freudian appears to think that, when instincts become aware of themselves, they control themselves.

This is absurd, and inconsistent with the Freudian theory of the Censor, a mysterious power in the mind which prevents it from being aware of the working of its instincts. Clearly, instincts, by themselves, are not capable of consciousness ; something else must be conscious, or unconscious, of them. You may, as some psychologists do, deny consciousness altogether ; but you cannot impute it to instinct nor can you hold that it is caused by instincts working in concert or conflict with each other. Consciousness is consciousness of their concert or conflict ; it is something which can control their concert or conflict; and we have never heard yet of an effect that can control its cause. The practical appeal of the Freudians is always to consciousness; they imply that it has the power to control instinct and so that it is something over and above instinct. Even while they tell us that we are all sex, they hope, by telling us that, to give us control of sex in the interests of the self; they do not mean that we should immediately proceed to act as sexual machines.

III

There is a class of theories about the nature of mind which may be called suicidal—they are like the pig, which is said to cut its own throat by swimming; for they attack the validity of all mental processes, including those which produce them. Thus, if everything in the mind is caused by instinct; if all morals come of the gregarious instinct and all art of the sexual; if our value for what we call righteousness and beauty is really only these two instincts giving themselves fine names to satisfy some further and self-deceiving instinct, the nature and purpose of which no one can explain, then intellectual processes also are subject to the same explanation, and that which we call our value for truth is but an instinct giving itself a fine name. Truth, then,

125

is a figment of the self-deceiving instinct, like righteousness and beauty ; and there is no more validity in the intellectual process than in the moral or æsthetic. But, if that is so, then, since it is the intellectual process which produces the theory, the theory itself is discredited with all that it discredits. A Frèudian could not continue to be a theorist at all if he held that conviction of truth is caused, as he holds moral conviction to be, by some instinct which transforms itself in consciousness into that conviction. He must reserve the intellectual activity from his destructive analysis, or the analysis also is destroyed by itself.

In practice, of course, he does reserve it, does hold that there is such a thing as truth to be discovered by the human mind, since he tries to discover it. While he may contend that all morals are to be explained in terms of the gregarious instinct, or all art in terms of the sexual, he does not explain his own theories in terms of any instinct. They are to him the truth ; and truth means to all of us a belief that is in accordance with the facts and has no unconscious cause. Indeed, the moment we become aware of an unconscious cause for any belief of our own or of others, it is discredited for us, just as morals are discredited when we see them to be a product of the gregarious instinct.

Evil and the New Psychology

As I began by saying—the way to destroy
a belief is to discover its cause. But if the
integrity of the intellectual activity must be
maintained, why not the integrity of the moral
and æsthetic activities ? If there is such a
thing as truth which can be directly perceived
by the mind, why are not righteousness and
beauty also to be directly perceived ? Why
not attempt, with regard to these also, a reconciliation between theory and practice ? Such
a reconciliation is now most urgently needed ;
for we are all troubled, consciously or unconsciously, by a misgiving that our judgments of
value lack the validity of our judgments of
fact ; that they are the effects of mechanical
causes ; and that if we could understand how
they were caused, they would lose their peculiar validity for us, and we should lose the
convictions that give life all its meaning. So
long as we have this misgiving, the passion
for truth seems the enemy of the passion for
righteousness and beauty ; and if that is so,
then are we of all creatures the most miserable.

But there is, I believe, the promise of a
reconciliation in that very discovery which to
the Freudians seems to establish the automatic
nature of mind ; for what it does establish is
the fact that all three spiritual activities of the
mind are alike subject to disorders mechanically caused ; in fact, that evil is so caused in

all its forms. It does not establish the fact that good is so caused ; indeed, instead of reducing good and evil both to the same mechanical process, it points to a new distinction between them, and one that gives us a new hope of mastering evil.

The words cause and effect are dangerous to thought, because we think that we understand their meaning when we do not. I will not, therefore, say that evil is caused and good is not ; but rather that evil, in the mind, is something of which a definite and immediate cause can be discovered, and which can often be removed by the discovery of that cause ; whereas good is something of which no definite or immediate cause can be discovered. This difference is hard to understand, and the difficulty has expressed itself in the dilemma of free will and predestination. Men have always seen, more or less dimly, the causes of the wrong processes of the mind, and so have inclined, when they thought of these, to determinism ; but they have also failed to see any causes of the right processes of the mind ; and, when they have thought of these, have inclined to a belief in the freedom of the will. In fact, the mind *is* like a machine when it acts wrongly, but not when it acts rightly.

But in the past there have been very strong practical causes for the assumption that the mind is in all things like a machine; since, proceeding on that assumption, men have found a cure or a palliative for many of the evils to which the mind is subject. So long as all kinds of wrong conduct, or even wrong belief, were held to be the expression of an evil will subject to no causes outside itself, there was no way of dealing with them except by punishment, which was usually itself a mechanical reaction and blind in its effects. But, as soon as wrong conduct and wrong belief were seen to have causes that can be discovered, their causes were sought, and sometimes found, with the best results. The new psychology is based on the assumption, constantly confirmed by experience, that there are causes for all error and evil in the mind; and its great discovery is that the mind, when aware of these causes, will, with the whole of itself, resist and often overcome them.

But that is no reason why it should slip into the further assumption that what is good in the mind is caused in the same way as what is evil; or should, in older terms, utterly deny the freedom of the will. Rather, we should look to the new psychology to illustrate both freedom and the lack of it; for, hard as it is to understand, or even to state the fact, both freedom and the lack of it seem to exist. It is only in theory that we ever think of discovering the causes of good. The practice of mankind is to take good for granted, as something that of its nature needs no explanation. But the same practice seeks an explanation of evil; for evil is that which ought not to be, that which instantly arouses in us the desire to remove it. There is, in fact, a problem of evil but, in the nature of things, no problem of good. The word provoked by evil is, why? but that word is never provoked by good. Good is identical with the self unified in a right relation, or answer, to external circumstances. But evil seems to be the self losing its unity, its identity, under a tyranny of external circumstances which turns it into a machine. Always when we are aware of evil in ourselves or in others, we are aware of the mechanical or automatic; the pain of evil consists in this, that it makes the self seem to itself a machine out of order. But it never seems to itself a machine in order, when it acts rightly. The sense of the mechanical, the caused, in the human mind is itself a sense of evil; and to import it also into good is to deny the difference between them.

According to the Freudians themselves, consciousness is good and unconsciousness evil, which means that automatism in the mind is evil, and something else—which we may call, vaguely enough, life or freedom—is good.

Evil and the New Psychology

But when we say that consciousness is good and unconsciousness evil, we need to know more precisely what we mean by those words, There is a sense in which the unconscious is not evil at all, but a necessary part of every mind ; though in this sense also the word is still vaguely used. But when the Freudian speaks of the unconscious as the enemy, he means the unconscious as a deceiver : means certain instincts disguising themselves in the conscious, so that it takes them for something other than they are. In that case, of course, consciousness is imperfect. If it were perfect, it would see through the disguise ; and the effort of the psycho-analyst is to make it more perfect, so that it can see through the disguise. Evil of all kinds—error, fear, hatred, all that makes for madness—thrives like a bacillus in the darkness of the mind ; when the light of consciousness is turned upon it, it ceases to thrive.

IV

Here, it might seem, we are back at the old barren and unconvincing simplification of evil into ignorance, and good into knowledge. But the discovery of the new psychology is of value, both practically and theoretically, because it avoids that simplification while doing justice to knowledge. The word con-

scious is misleading, because it seems to mean
a purely intellectual process; but, in fact,
when a man becomes aware of the cause of
error, or of any other evil in his mind, the
process by which he overcomes that evil is
more than intellectual. The awareness of evil,
in proportion to its completeness and precision,
causes the whole mind to mobilize against the
evil, to unify itself against that danger which
threatens its unity.

Where the unity of the mind is impaired
by any evil within it, whether sin or error, it
is filled with a sense of impotence, and of
automatism; it begins at once to believe
about itself that which will become true if the
evil persists and increases. And the more
completely it is unconscious of the evil and of
its cause, the more automatic and impotent
it seems to itself. But consciousness of the
evil and of its cause at once gives the mind
confidence in its own unity and power; there
is some joy even in the agonies of repentance,
because repentance means an access, however
imperfect, of consciousness, and so of the sense
of power. And what is repentance or conviction of sin but the beginning, at least, of that
consciousness which, according to the new
psychology, is the healer of the mind? Men
do get strength from confession because it
forces them to state their sin in plain terms;

Evil and the New Psychology

it is the beginning of the process which the psycho-analyst tries to complete. And when Plato said that the lie of the soul was the worst of all lies, he meant the lie with which the unconscious deceives the conscious, the lie which makes men behave automatically while they think they are behaving like rational creatures.

Perhaps the greatest and most dangerous of all human errors is the belief that we are, always and in all respects, alive ; that we have been born alive and must remain so until we die. For, in fact, the living part of us, both physical and mental, is always liable to be overcome by a mechanical process, like those processes to which inorganic matter is subject. Just as our minds still have in them a brutishness inherited from the past, so our very life seems to inherit habits from the inorganic matter out of which it has arisen ; and because of this inheritance, it is always, more or less, imperfectly life.

The body, for instance, is subject to strange automatisms of disease, in which a purposeless growth destroys its life ; and madness is an automatism of the mind, in which instincts behave as if they really were forces, and the unconscious masters the conscious.

This invasion and conquest of life by not-life is what we mean by evil, whether it takes the form of disease, of error, of sin, or of æsthetic perversity. In fact, the difference between evil and good is not less, but far greater than we ever dreamed it was; for it is the difference, in a living creature, between life and not-life. And our profound hatred and fear of evil, so far from being a matter of consciousness only, is life's hatred and fear of a threatening and invasive not-life. We feel that hatred and fear with the whole living part of ourselves; but the more evil masters us, the more are that hatred and fear weakened with the life which is being overcome by not-life. Hence the close connexion between error and sin and æsthetic perversity; they are all symptoms of not-life, of automatism mastering life. It is because we suppose that we are always and in all respects alive, that we have failed to see the identity between life and good, and between evil and not-life. We cannot think of life as identical with good so long as we believe that we are always fully alive; for we know that we are not always completely good. And while we know that good is a matter of quality, we suppose life to be a matter of quantity, to be merely something that is or is not.

But, in fact, the very essence of life is its effort to be more intensely life; and the struggle for life is not merely a struggle of

life to maintain itself against external dangers :
it is also, and still more, an internal struggle.
Life is always fighting for its life against a
tendency within itself to behave as if it were
not-life ; and it is this struggle, carried on in
purely physical terms in the lower forms of
life, that becomes, in the higher, moral, intellectual, æsthetic, without ceasing to be still a
struggle of life against not-life.

That which we call the spirit of man, that
which distinguishes him from the beasts, is a
higher quality, a greater intensity, of life ;
but this greater intensity never escapes from
the struggle with automatisms. The musician
composing a melody must resist them ; only,
the more completely he is an artist, the more
fully is he aware of their danger. And that
is true also of the saint and the philosopher.
Bad art, bad thinking, wrong conduct, all
these are relapses into automatism. In the
midst of life we are in death more profoundly
than we ever have supposed.

The Manichæans, when they said that matter
was evil, had a glimmering of the truth, for
they saw that evil was not something inherent
in the spirit of life. But they were wrong in
making the final distinction between matter
and spirit. The final distinction is between
life and not-life. In fact, the issue between
good and evil, so far from being confused by

the discoveries of the new psychology, is made sharper and more momentous than it ever was before. All forms of evil are allied, as being automatisms ; and all forms of good, as being manifestations and efforts of life. Psychology itself, when it is real psychology, is not merely a curiosity which may discover ugly truths about the mind, and which may, therefore, be the enemy of our moral and æsthetic values. It is also part of the effort of life to be more intensely life, to extend that consciousness which is more alive than unconsciousness.

So long as we think of the struggle for life as being purely instinctive or automatic, there will seem to us to be a conflict, which never can be reconciled, between that struggle and the higher activities of man ; but this sense of a conflict that cannot be reconciled is only a modern form of Manichæism. As soon as the struggle for life becomes to us a struggle against automatism, a struggle for quality rather than quantity of life, we escape from the Manichæan sense of an irreconcilable conflict. The instinct of self-preservation, when it acts against the higher activities of the spirit, becomes for us, not the struggle for life, but a mere automatism, which life itself must resist. And so it is with all the other instincts : they are not evil, as the Manichæans held, nor are they irresistible forces behind the con-

Evil and the New Psychology

sciousness which, to flatter itself, it calls by pretty names. But they are liable to become automatic, when the consciousness fails to control them; and it can control them only by being aware of them. So the awareness at which the psycho-analyst aims is part of the effort of life to preserve itself from automatism, to make the whole mind alive and so good.

Some may fear that this identification of good with life, and of evil with not-life, will destroy for us the reality of the distinction between good and evil. Any theory which does that is malign, and sure, sooner or later, to be condemned by the judgment of mankind. For, in fact, no distinction is so real to us as that between good and evil; and, if we lost it, we should lose all sense of our own identity. Yes, but our sense of our own identity, so bound up with our sense of the difference between good and evil, *is* our sense of life. For life does not mean in fact, as it often means in talk, some vague common stock, which we all share. It means the individual self, and it exists only in individual selves. Life, in fact, *is* differentiation; the greater the intensity of life, the more differentiation there is; and that is true also of all kinds of good. There is a common stock of bad poetry, but the good poem says one thing as only it can be said. Our sense of its goodness is a sense

of differentiation from all other poems ; and,
when we have said that it is good, we are apt
to add also that it is alive.

Automatism to us, in poetry and all art,
means commonplace, deadness, badness. And
so it is with conduct. We are aware of a
sameness in all kinds of wickedness. Milton's
Satan is not evil as it is, but evil glorified by
the expression of a great poet. In evil, as we
really meet it, there is something dull and
generic, rather than specific and brilliant ; it
is mechanical, automatic action, without regard
to the particular facts. A man subject to lust
or rage or egotism becomes a machine, and
behaves like all other men subject to the same
passions. We see in him the passions, not
himself ; and what horrifies us in wickedness,
besides its effects, is this dying of life out of
the human being, this horrible marionettism
pretending to be life. Whenever we hate a
man, he has ceased to be himself to us, and
become generic, typical of some automatism,
while we ourselves, in that hatred, are also
invaded by automatism. And it is the same
with thought : error has always something
generic in it, while truth is specific ; for error
is automatism pretending to be thought and
repeating itself in formulæ ; while truth is
that particular truth and no other.

Until we identify life with good, life is not

Evil and the New Psychology

completely life to us ; nor is good completely
good. The identification throws light on both
of them, like the identification of God with love.
So long as we think of life as not being necessarily and altogether good, we suppose that
those automatisms which attack it belong to
it ; and so long as we think of good as something different from life, we are not altogether
in love with it, but suppose that it may be
dull and monotonous. So there are people who
imagine that saints are unpleasant, or that
classical music has no melody, or that all
truths are unwelcome. To them good is
something not quite alive ; and they may
even be drawn to evil because they suppose
it to be more alive than good. So their sense
of the difference between good and evil is
actually weakened by their failure to identify
good with life and evil with not-life.

And, finally, there is this failure in the
perversities of the new psychology. If the
Freudian saw that good was life and evil not-
life, he would see that the analysis which he
can apply to evil in the mind cannot also be
applied to good. For that analysis is itself
part of the effort which life makes to rid itself
of not-life. Good, that is life, the unified self,
cannot analyse itself ; it can only analyse the
automatisms which threaten its unity. When
it tries to analyse itself also into automatisms,

it is becoming automatic ; and nothing could
be more automatic than some of the assumptions of the Freudians. So long as they deal
with evil they are men of science, and there
is the life of thought in them ; but, as soon
as they try to subject the whole content of
the mind to their analysis, the life dies out
of their thinking, and they repeat formulæ,
unconfirmed by experience. At one moment
Freud is a man of genius, is himself, and no
one else, in an eager, living pursuit of truth ;
at the next, he is mastered by an unconscious
assumption and becomes a Freudian.

The practical task of psychology is always,
in a sense, negative ; it is to remove from the
mind obstacles to its own vital process. In
that it is like all medicine, the task of which
is, not to make health, but to remove obstacles
to it. Just as medicine can discover the causes
of disease, but not the causes of health, of
wrong relations between the body and its
environment, but not of right, so psychology
can analyse, and remove by its analysis, all
that makes for automatism in the mind, but
not the life of the mind. And that is the
practice of the Freudian, whatever his theory
may be. He puts his faith in the life of the
mind, when he has exposed its automatisms
by analysis ; and it is the underlying principle
of all psycho-analysis that the final appeal

Evil and the New Psychology

must be to the life of the mind by making it aware of its automatisms. That life, that unity, that consciousness, or conscience, is there, to be strengthened by external help, but not to be explained by the same process that explains and destroys the unconscious automatism, evil. For, even if it could be so explained, there would finally be nothing for the psychoanalyst to appeal to, no difference between good and evil, between life and not-life.

VI

The Nature of Evil ∽　∽　∽

GOOD AS LIFE—EVIL AS NOT-LIFE

THE words good and evil express the most extreme opposites that our minds are able to conceive; in fact no other difference is of any importance to us compared with the difference between them, and all our final judgments are in terms of them. Yet they have this at least in common, that they can happen only to living things. The simplest form of good is physical pleasure; the simplest form of evil is physical pain; both consist of sensation and there cannot be sensation without life. Things may happen to a stone; but, if they produce no sensation, they can be neither good nor evil to it. So, in a universe without life, things might happen, forces might be at work, the stars might move in their courses, but it would be empty alike of good and of evil.

Further, as good and evil cannot exist without life, so with every increase of life there is a larger capacity for the experience of both good and evil. Life means a contact with external things different in kind from the contact of which things not living are capable ; for with life comes a response to contact which we call sensation, and every increase of life means an increase of response. The first response is to touch and is of one sense only, namely the sense of touch. Then, as other senses are developed, there comes a diversity of response, with a diversity of contact. And out of that comes a unity both of contact and of response, namely perception, which is a use of different senses in combination by means of which the living creature becomes aware, not only of its own sensations,—not merely of feeling, seeing, smelling, or hearing—but of an object felt, seen, smelt and heard ; and with this awareness of an object comes the sense of evil as well as of pain. Animals are aware of objects evil to them which they hate or fear ; and the more intelligent of them can find evil in an object, whether living or not living, and remember the evil, manifesting hate or fear when they see the object again. This remembrance we may call the beginning of the sense of evil as something over and above pleasure or pain, and it comes with a fuller contact with the not-self, it is a more complex reaction of the living thing against that which is seen as in some way hostile to life.

*   *   *   *   *

If you begin to think about the nature of evil, you will find yourself sooner or later confronted with the problem of free will and predestination. You may try to evade it as being unreal as a ghost from the past ; but it is a ghost that refuses to be laid, and it is inseparable from the problem of evil for this reason : that if we did and suffered only good, we should never ask the question Are our wills free or are they not ? There would be always an identity between what we willed and what we did or what happened to us. It might seem inevitable, but, since we should never wish to avoid it, we should be aware of no compulsion in it. But evil is the same as compulsion to us ; because it happens and yet our will is against it, whenever we know it to be evil. Compulsion implies evil and evil implies compulsion ; and the problem of free will and predestination or necessity arises because evil exists as well as good. You will find, if you examine your own thought and feeling, that predestination, necessity, call it what you will, means to you the being compelled to something contrary to your own will or desire. If it is what you desire— whether it be something that happens to you from outside, or something that happens in your own body, such as physical pleasure, or something that you do—you do not think of it, except by some conscious philosophical effort,

The Nature of Evil

as you do not think of yourself as compelled.
People may talk of the chain of cause and effect,
but it is a chain to us only when we are constrained by it. At other times it is like the air
in which we live and move and have our being
freely.

In fact there are times when necessity and
our wills are at one, and then we seem to ourselves to be free; that is when good is happening to us and when we are doing good. But
there are also times when necessity and our
wills are in conflict. That is when evil happens
to us or we do evil, as it seems to us, because
something forces us to do it against our will.
Then it is that the problem of predestination
and free will arises, because we seem to be
aware of both, and because neither seems to
be supreme. For while evil may overcome us,
while it may seem to hold us in an iron chain
of cause and effect, yet it is evil that makes us
conscious of the will, since it provokes the will
to resist it. But when we experience good,
there is for us an identity of will and necessity
in which both are lost; and the greater the
good, the more complete this identity. There
is no compulsion and there is no effort, but a
harmony of ourselves and all things in which we
have our part, both willed and necessary as if
they were notes in a tune. Then necessity is the
highest good; and good seems all the more

good because it is necessary and could not be otherwise. In fact at our moments of greatest happiness we could, like Leonardo da Vinci, write hymns to necessity as being identical with good; and then, paradoxically, evil seems to us that which is not necessary, and the problem of evil becomes this: Why is it that that which is not necessary, that which ought not to be, yet compels us to acknowledge its existence?

Certainly, in fact, we do not regard evil as necessary, since our natural response to it is to resist it. The problem of evil is to us always and first of all a practical problem. The question it provokes is, How is it to be avoided or destroyed? It is only when we fail to avoid or destroy it that the energy at once provoked and thwarted by it expresses itself in the further question, Why does evil exist? If we could always overcome evil, we should persist in overcoming it until it existed no longer, and then we should not have to ask the question, Why does it exist?

So the problem of free will and predestination is only one form of the question provoked by evil when we cannot overcome it. The question is not really, are we free or are we predestined? but rather, Why is there sometimes an identity between necessity and our wills and sometimes a discord so that we are aware of compulsion? The identity is good and the discord evil. And the problem of predestination and free will belongs not so much to philosophy as to myth. It is a representation, in other terms, of a conflict always happening in our lives. Now we are free, now compelled. We have not to make a choice between the two theories, to decide whether we are free or compelled; for, in fact, we are now one, now the other; and this fact bewilders us so much that we have great difficulty in stating it at all.

Necessity, whenever we think of it as necessity, that is to say as compulsion, seems to us an evil thing; but, when we think of it as what we ourselves will and desire, happening because it must, then it is to us complete and perfect good. The great religious teachers and visionaries have always spoken of a higher necessity which they call the Will of God and to which man may also attain. For them the alternatives of free will and necessity only exist where there is evil in the mind of man. It is evil *which is not necessary but compelling* that provokes will; and will may be itself evil, may take sides with this compelling but not necessary evil against the true and higher necessity that is the Will of God. In any case will, when we are aware of it and its struggle with compulsion, implies evil not overcome. And so long as we are aware of will, we are not free. We attain to freedom, as Leonardo also said, only in a complete identity between our wills and the higher necessity. Hence the saying of St. Augustine : " Restless are our hearts until they rest in Thee " ; and the saying of Dante : " In His will is our peace."

These sayings of theirs I mention here only as methods of expression. They may not be true, but they are in any case psychologically interesting, as examples of the manner in which the problem of evil has presented itself to certain great minds. In some way they are denials of the reality of evil. Good to them is the will of God, is necessity, is reality. Evil is something that exists, but it is not necessity or reality ; for them as for all men it is that which must be overcome.

That is really the very definition of evil, a definition which at once concerns, not only the nature of evil, but our relation to it. *It is something which exists to be overcome.* And, in fact, it would be impossible to think of evil at all without thinking of our relation to it, or to define it except in terms of our relation to it. For if there were no life evil could not be. It exists because life exists, like good ; but whereas good is something we can contemplate without the thought of action—and the very contemplation of it is also good to us—evil does always provoke us, not to contemplation, but to action, namely to the overcoming of it. If we concern ourselves with evil at all, even if we think about its nature, we have always and necessarily a practical purpose, namely to overcome it. The pure contemplation of evil would no doubt be evil if it were possible, but it is not possible. Though evil is what makes us aware of necessity in the form of compulsion, though it is that which causes us to doubt the freedom of the will, yet it also provokes us to deny its necessity in the most practical manner, since it provokes the will to overcome it.

It is possible for us to forget this fact in our thought about evil, because when we think about a thing we may be tempted by the difficulties of thought to think away from the thing; we may, in our desire to reach some conclusion about it, empty it, for purposes of thought, of its very nature. And we are tempted so to empty evil of its very nature because it is something that baffles us the moment we try to think of it. It seems indeed to refuse to be thought about, as if it has the power of infecting our mental processes with itself and making us stupid and afraid. And that is because the very existence of evil is intolerable to us in thought. If we try to understand its nature, another question springs up and confuses our thought—namely the question, Why does evil exist at all. Why? Why? Why? This question, as I have already said, is the result of our failure to overcome evil, it is the expression of a thwarted energy. Presenting itself as so urgent, yet offering no hope of an answer, it is itself part of the pain of evil.

We can escape from it and the pain of it, we can prevent it from confusing our thought, only if we remember always that the proper aim of that thought is always practical, namely to overcome evil. That is to say, we must never think about evil as if it were not evil, not something to be overcome, as if it *could* be the subject of disinterested contemplation. If we do that, we are lying to ourselves about it ; we are emptying it of its very nature in order that we may think about it ; and we are thinking about something which has no existence.

The history of thought and of religion proves that it is very necessary to insist upon this. Because the existence of evil is intolerable to the mind of man : because the question, Why does it exist ? is itself painful (being the result of vain effort to overcome evil), men have always been tempted to evade it by trying in some way to persuade themselves that evil does not exist. And this they do by asserting that it is not entirely different from good, that it is good in some disguised form. But when they think about an evil that is not entirely different from good, it is not evil they think about. And further the universe they think about, in which

evil is, not itself, but disguised universal good,
may be more intelligible than the real universe,
but it is not one which exists. They are like
the bad lawyer who always tells you what the
law would be if the facts were different ; they
may solve a problem, but it is not the one set
by reality.

This, however, happens so often in thought
about evil that there must be some powerful
cause for it, of which the thinkers are themselves unaware. And the cause is, I think, that
they hope to endure evil better if they can persuade themselves that it is not really evil, not
utterly different from good, but rather an, to
us, unintelligible variety of good, which, if we
could understand it, we should value, and perhaps even enjoy. Therefore they try to understand it in those terms and so, really, to supply
themselves with an anæsthetic against evil.

That this is the cause of the effort to mini-
mize the difference between evil and good, is
proved, I think, by the fact that men were
making that effort long before they began to
philosophize at all. All religions in their
infancy, and many in their maturity, maintain
that both good and evil come from God, and
that evil therefore is to be patiently endured as
having a divine origin and a divine purpose.
This view of evil persists even in the Litany of
the Church of England :

"Remember not, Lord, our offences, nor the offences of our forefathers ; neither take thou vengeance of our sins. Spare us, good Lord, spare Thy people, whom Thou hast redeemed with thy most precious blood, and be not angry with us for ever."

Here evil is not something to be resisted and overcome, but something to be deprecated and endured, because, like good, it comes from God. And the notion that it comes from God has led even Christians to impute to God Himself evil passions such as anger, evil motives such as vengeance, and evil actions such as injustice. This is what always happens where evil is, like good, imputed to God ; the God Himself becomes evil ; and the results are seen in the actions of men. ·

That, no doubt is why religion has so often persuaded men to evil. For if once you believe that your God consents to evil of any kind, that, like the Jesuits according to the Protestant view of them, He does evil that good may come, you are in danger of worshipping not a god but a devil ; and in many primitive religions there is no difference between God and devil, or between godlike and devilish behaviour in his worshippers. Moloch was God and devil in one, and men sacrificed their children to him, because in their effort to reconcile themselves to evil they had come to believe that their God could will it. Behind all religious perversion there is the attempt to be reconciled to evil so that it may be better endured ; and that attempt is itself the extreme example of perversion, leading as it does to the most monstrous perversities of thought and feeling and conduct.

But these perversities are not necessarily connected with religion ; they occur also in those who have long ceased to believe in any kind of God, but who still try to reconcile themselves to evil as a variety of good—especially when it is evil that happens to others. Thus to-day there are those who believe in the value of ruthless competition and of war itself, as evils out of which good will come by a kind of mechanical process. True, they seem to employ reason to justify their belief ; where once men talked of the will of God, they talk of the process of evolution and the survival of the fittest ; but their reason is merely rationalizing which conceals from themselves the cause of their perversity, namely their desire to make terms with evil so that it may be endured rather than overcome.

There have also been many philosophic attempts to make terms with evil ; and their method is usually to pass, unnoticed by the philosopher himself, from metaphor into thought, thought into metaphor. Evil is necessary to good, is the correlative of good ; it is like the shadow without which there can be no light, the discord without which harmony would be insipid, the bitter that gives a relish to sweet. *But, in fact, evil is not in the least like any of these, for none of these are evil.* These metaphors could satisfy no one who was suffering from evil. No man suffering from pain has ever believed that without pain he could never have any pleasure. Try it on yourself when you have the toothache and you will see that it does not convince you or reconcile you to the toothache. No man repenting of a sin has ever believed that his virtues could not exist without his vices. We are told that, if we could see the whole, we should see that there was no evil; but when we suffer evil, we feel it is an obstacle, not merely to our vision of the whole, but to the very existence of a whole; it is something violating the unity of the universe, as sin violates the unity of the self.

So both in theory and in practice we must refuse to make terms with evil. We cannot think rightly about it or act rightly against it, unless it is *always* for us evil, a thing to be opposed and, if possible, overcome. It may be necessary to endure some particular evil—what can't be cured must be endured, as we say—but this endurance must not pervert our thought about it. We must begin and end by seeing it as in all things the opposite of good. The word

The Nature of Evil

itself has come into being to express the fact that there is this opposite of good, this something with which our only concern is to overcome it. It is the product of ages of experience, and that experience cannot be contradicted by any ingenuities of thought. But evil would not be entirely evil if it had not the power of overcoming us, by deceiving us about its very nature, by tempting us to make terms with it. There is indeed a logic in the very principle of evil; it is that which confuses and bewilders us when we think about it, unless we keep the logic of its nature always in mind—unless, that is, we insist in our thought that it is in every respect the opposite of good. The right attitude to evil is in the words, "Resist the Devil and he will flee from you"; and there must be the same resistance in our thought about evil or it will suffer quick perversion.

That this resistance is difficult is proved by our legends about the Devil himself. They tend to romanticize him; and they betray a tendency to romanticize evil, that is to say, to invest it with some of the qualities of good. Thus Milton's Satan is far from being all evil; he is heroic, defiant, full at least of life. But a true devil, if it were possible to personify evil at all, would be life automatized; he would talk, not with the eloquence of Milton's Satan, but like a leading article in a newspaper advocating some iniquity in a series of moral platitudes. To romanticize him, to invest him even with beauties of expression, would be to misrepresent evil; and Milton does that when he accepts the myth that Satan is a fallen angel.

There is in evil no angelic past or trace of ruined splendour. The Devil is a kind of imitation god, not an imitation of a real God, but an expression of wrong notions about God. He is that which men worship when they waste their divine faculties upon an unreality; and he is worshipped by all those who would make terms with evil so that they may the better endure it. But this we can understand only if we see evil always as the very opposite of good. If good in its utmost intensity is to us personal, is God, then evil is not personal, is not even a fallen angel, but the opposite and the enemy of all personality and all life. If good is beauty, then evil is ugliness; the complete ugliness that comes, not of perverted character but of lack of character, the ugliness that is failure of expression disguising itself in platitude.

Evil, as we know it in ourselves, has always this power of disguise, this imitative and parasitic power of disguise; its very nature is to pretend to be what it is not; and our concern with it is to separate ourselves from it, by seeing through its disguises. For this we need

The Nature of Evil

all our faculties, intellectual and æsthetic as well as moral ; above all we need the new weapon of psychology which, if it fulfils its promise, may become for us an Ithuriel's spear. When the Devil within us pretends to be an angel of light, when our stupidity seems wisdom, when our automatism seems life, at a touch of that spear the disguise will fall away and we shall be aware of the enemy within ourselves, the not-self pretending to be the self, mechanism pretending to be life, the evil which will no longer persuade us to make terms with it.

We are still far from that happy state ; but we are at least beginning to see that some day it may be possible ; and in this essay I attempt to forecast that possibility. But we must start with the axiom that evil is that which is in all respects different from good, and that our concern with it is always practical, namely to overcome it.

VII

The English Bible ᴑ   ᴑ   ᴑ

IT is hard for us to take any book that has
become a classic quite seriously, and
hardest of all to take the Bible so. We
can take a book just written seriously because
we have no preconceptions about it. We do
not feel bound to think that it is all true ; nor
do we react against those who insist that it is
all true. We can allow for the circumstances
that affect the author's thought ; whether he
seems right or wrong, we can sympathize with
him and make allowances for him.

But some people read the Bible now because
they believe it is all absolutely true ; others
for the " poetry " in it ; others as an interesting
relic of the past ; others because they wish to
find the best defence for it they can ; others
because they wish to attack it. And none of
these takes it quite seriously. If you believe
that a book with so many inconsistencies in it
is all true, you cannot believe that it means
all that it says. You make it mean what you
choose ; and that it is not taking it seriously. If

you read it all for its poetry, you read a great
part of it for what it was not meant to be,
and you cannot really understand the poetry
unless you know what the writer was trying to
do. If it is to you an interesting relic of the
past, it has no present application; the very
men who wrote it are to you mere curiosities,
While, if you wish to defend or attack it, you
look only for what you can attack or defend.

The way to take the Bible seriously is to
understand that those who wrote it were dealing with problems that we have to deal with
now. They were men like ourselves, not
angels, not mere savages; they were in a state
neither of invincible ignorance nor of invincible
omniscience. They were not utterly right nor
utterly perverse. You cannot see the immense
value, beauty, truth, passion of the Bible unless
you rid your mind of all those preconceptions
that will destroy its alertness. It is not that
you need to be critical; critical, that is, of
other people's ideas about the Bible. What
you need is to take it so seriously as to forget
other people's ideas about it; to see it as the
work of men who really were labouring to say
something; and to try yourself, without prejudice, to understand what they were labouring
to say. And it is necessary, first of all, to get
rid of the notion that they were all trying to
" edify." Isaiah was not trying to edify.

When he said, "Hear, O heavens, and give ear, O earth," he meant that he had something to say which he must say, just as we say, "Listen to me." It was not egotism ; it was the sense that he was possessed by an absolute truth which he must utter because it was truth. He was, as we say, bursting with it ; and his very manner of speech is the manner of a man bursting with it. Further, he spoke it to the people of his own times, threatened with particular dangers and guilty of particular crimes and follies. He spoke to them with a particular object, and not to a remote posterity in general poetic language. That is why he is so real. But we cannot see the reality of him unless we take him seriously enough to see how he took himself.

Then there is St. Paul. How few of those who praise or condemn him, take him seriously enough to regard him as a real man, dealing with real immediate problems, whether of thought or of policy. They suppose that he had made up his mind, rightly or wrongly, about everything from the first, and that he wrote merely to express one clear unalterable system, whether inspired or nonsensical. But no one who takes him seriously enough to read him with attention can believe that. He is evidently, like all real thinkers and actors, a discoverer and breathless with the ardour of

discovery, too breathless to be dignified. " I
am debtor both to the Greeks, and to the
Barbarians ; both to the wise, and to the un-
wise." He was a debtor to every moment of
his experience, to every practical problem he
had to solve. Life to him meant learning, and
that was why it meant teaching. He writes
to put down what has just struck him ; and it
came to him out of his immediate experience,
So you must dramatize him, as it were, to
understand him ; and that means that you must
take him as seriously as you take yourself.
There is a strange stupidity in those who jibe
at St. Paul, the stupidity of a complete lack of
sympathy. He is not a man to them, but an
institution which they wish to abolish. But
that is because to many of his admirers also he
has been merely an institution. They have
robbed him of humanity to praise him. They
have refused to see him in all his circumstances
of time and place, and so they have not seen
him at all.

But why, when there is the real man to
understand and learn from, should we react
against this stupidity with equal stupidity ?
It is the stupidity of those who will not enjoy
Shakespeare because of all the nonsense that
has been written in praise of him. Why cut
off your nose to spite some one else's face ?
There is the beauty and passion of the mind of

man, of the universe, to be shared by you, to be made your own. Why shut yourself off from it one way because others have shut themselves off from it another way ? Some men are too much afraid of losing faith, others of finding it. Both fail to take the Bible seriously and miss much by their failure.

The Authorized Version of the Bible is a piece of literature without any parallel in modern times. Other countries, of course, have their translations of the Bible, but they are not great works of art. The only other translation that can be compared with the Authorized Version is the Vulgate ; and that is written in a language now foreign to everybody. We cannot understand the nature and value of its influence unless we also understand something of the process by which it came to be what it is, unless we realize that it is more than a translation, that it expresses the religious thoughts and emotions of Englishmen as well as of Jews and early Christians.

It could not do this if it had been made, as most books are made, in a few years and by one man. It was more than 200 years in the making, and many minds had a part in it. The Middle Ages were in their decadence when Wyclif began it ; the Renaissance was changing quickly into the modern world when it

was finished. In this period of transition it
was accomplished while many things of great
beauty and value were being destroyed ; and
it has proved itself a substitute for some of the
best of these, perhaps the only substitute the
modern world has produced. In the Middle
Ages religion had a splendid and highly organ-
ized means of expression in architecture and
all its subsidiary arts. Then the great Cathe-
drals rose by the labour of many hands and of
many minds. Not one of them was the work
of a single man, and each profited by the
experience and discoveries of the past. The
Cathedral builders did not try to be original ;
their only aim was to improve upon the work
of their predecessors; and so it was with the
series of translators of the Bible. They began,
as we have said, when the Middle Ages were
declining with all their institutions, with their
Church and all its manifold arts ; and in the
end they gave us the written word instead of
the word in pictures and sculpture and build-
ing. In no other nation was the same feat
accomplished. Germany and France have
their national epics ; but they were made
before the modern world began, and they are
not religious. So they are no substitutes for
the great religious arts of the Middle Ages.
They are kept alive mainly by patriotism and
literary piety. Sayings from them are not

constantly in the mouths of the people ; nor are they read aloud weekly in any kind of assembly. We alone have the good fortune to possess Scriptures which are thus familiar to us all, and at the same time full of a beauty which our own tongue has given to them and of a poetry which expresses our faith. Whatever changes in that faith there may have been, the Bible is not obsolete, even for the most free-thinking among us ; indeed it is less obsolete than Shakespeare himself. In its vast diversity it has matter for every kind of mind and for every period of life, and all this matter is expressed in language of such beauty and simplicity that its effect is not weakened by any changes of taste. The words " And God said, Let there be light : and there was light," still sound as sublime to us as they sounded to Longinus, who first quoted them as an example of sublimity. In the Song of Solomon all the passion of the East is naturalized among us. There are the Proverbs to be quoted, like Horace, for their worldly wisdom. There is Ecclesiastes, full of the ancient weariness of life which still comes to those who are sated with pleasure and see nothing beyond it. There is the story of Joseph for romance, told as Tolstoy would have told it yesterday ; and there is Psalm cxxvi to express for every one the quiet joy,

sweeter for the bitterness remembered in it,
that comes after long sorrow : " They that
sow in tears shall reap in joy." The metaphor
is one that binds all ages and races together ;
but the words are ours and make us think of
our own native fields and harvests, and they
contain a truth that is true to all of us who
have any kind of faith whatsoever.

The Bible is to us what Homer was to the
Greeks. We know it as well as they knew
Homer ; and, like Homer, it has for us that universal and enduring sanctity with which familiarity invests only the greatest things. And it is
no small privilege that we should thus be forced
from our earliest years into this familiarity with
a work of such diverse and exalted beauty.
Every one who has known the Bible from
infancy is as fortunate as a child born and
nurtured in a beautiful city and under the
shadow of a great church. Unconsciously he
has received into his mind memories that will
enrich it for the rest of his life. These memories could not be so strong and sweet as they
are, if our Bible were only a translation and
not glorified with all the arts of our own
language. We think of its stories as happening
in England, of Ruth as standing in tears amid
no alien corn, because the translators have
made these stories their own and ours, expressing their feelings in them as fully and directly

as if there had been no original text to control
them. In fact, they have done for us in
words what so many of the earlier Italian
painters did for their countrymen in pictures.
They have made the Bible real for us without
making it trivial, by turning it into an English
book ; so that we can without any incongruity
make pictures out of it in our minds full of
English things. This we do in childhood, and
the pictures remain with us for the rest of
our lives, glorified by association with the
language that first begot them.

This is an æsthetic education of the best
kind, because it is easy, natural, and not merely
æsthetic. It gives us a chance at least of
acquiring the purity of taste, that delight in
simple immemorial things, without which it is
difficult for men to be good and impossible for
their goodness to be persuasive. There are
not many means among us now of producing
the beauty of holiness ; but the Bible remains
the chief of them, because it connects holiness
with beauty more directly and more closely
than any other work of man. We may shudder
at the modern divorce between these two when
we look at many modern churches and chapels ;
we may even feel that there is a kind of blas-
phemy in accepting such wanton eye-sores for
places of worship ; but we must remember
that the Bible is still read aloud in them, and

affords beauty for the ear and mind where there is none for the eye. This beauty has existed even for the narrowest and sourest of our religious sects, to whom all other kinds of beauty seemed sinful or trifling. They would have protested, no doubt, that they valued the Bible only for its truth; yet the more they believed in its every word, the more powerfully, if unconsciously, must its beauty have affected them. The Puritans, no doubt, found excuses for their own savage instincts in many texts of the Old Testament. They did not understand that there was a moral obligation upon them to use their brains to the best of their ability in applying the lessons of the Bible to their own lives. But, however fierce and narrow and tyrannical, they certainly had a dignity of conduct and language which mere fanaticism would not have given to them. We have only to read the trials of the Regicides to see that they could comport themselves, not only bravely but grandly, when face to face with death in the midst of their foes. Even that ordeal had a romance for them, because they passed through it comparing themselves with prophets and saints. In fact, to them, and all the Puritan heroes of the Civil War and all the persecuted Covenanters after the Restoration, the Old Testament was just such an inspiration and a romance as the *Iliad* was

167

to Alexander. They thought of Joshua as he thought of Achilles, and their ambitions were as far removed from vulgarity as his.

Yet their belief in the verbal inspiration of the Bible and the evil effects of that belief caused a prejudice against Biblical quotations which has lasted to the present day. This prejudice is partly religious and partly social. There are some devout people who think that the Bible is too sacred a book to be quoted from freely. There are others, not devout, who think that to quote from it is a breach of good manners. Both of these notions arise from the idea that those who quote from it usually do so to suit their own purposes, and so take an unfair advantage of its sacred character. But there is little danger now of anyone being misled by a belief in its verbal inspiration. The danger rather is that it should become only a subject of special study, that it should be treated as a series of historical or literary documents to be read for some ulterior purpose, and not for its own sake. Now that we have so many cheap substitutes for literature it is more than ever necessary that every one from childhood should be familiar with the Bible, not as a book which proves something or which contains curious information, but as one which says what is best worth saying in the best possible words. Such a familiarity with

The English Bible

it ought to be considered the foundation of all
culture among us ; and we ought to learn it at
school as the Greeks learned Homer, and to be
able to quote from it without any false shame
and without suggesting any controversy about
theological matters. One may still meet old
peasant women who know it in this intimate
way and who quote from it aptly, not to prove
their own devoutness, but because it is their
one book and for them contains all the wisdom
of the world. Yet they are growing rarer, and
their children are more apt to read cheap
magazines, and papers, and to betray the
influence of these both in their speech and in
their thought. This is not to be wondered at,
for the children of the rich are in the same case.
They, too, know the Bible less than their
fathers knew it. If they are taught it at all,
they are not taught it disinterestedly. They
are made to read it for the information it
contains, and so that they may be able to
answer questions about it set in examinations.
To them the Bible often means a list of the
Kings of Israel and Judah, or the journeys of
St. Paul, which can be learnt in vile hexa-
meters, or the items peculiar to each of the
four Evangelists, all of which things can be
learnt without any study of the Bible itself,
and when learnt will not help the learner to
understand or enjoy it.

169

There is now so much subsidiary knowledge of a much more valuable kind to be acquired about the Bible that we are in danger of hiding the Bible itself in the surrounding thickets of that knowledge. We need to remember that it is knowledge for specialists, whereas every one ought to have a knowledge of the book. We can read Isaiah and enrich our minds with the glory of his language and his passion for righteousness without knowing how many Isaiahs there were, when they lived, or which of them wrote what part of the text. That is only the knowledge of curiosity; but to know the text itself is the knowledge of culture, the disinterested knowledge which every kind of mind requires. There is no fear now that we shall take anything in the Bible too literally. The fear rather is that we shall regard it as a mere pretext for the ingenuities of modern investigators, as the Baconians regard the text of Shakespeare as a mine of cryptograms. The investigators themselves can do no harm; but there is no reason why we should all know what they have discovered or conjectured. That is a kind of science of no great importance to the mass of men. It is important to every one to know the Bible from childhood, for there is no great literature in our own tongue, or perhaps in any other, which a child can so easily enjoy. Parts of it he will not under-

stand ; indeed, parts can only be understood
by those who have had a long and intense
experience of life ; and parts, of course, are
only of historical or other interest for specialists. But, of the rest, part has been handed
down from the childhood of the world and still
keeps its primeval freshness and glory like no
other writings in our language. The child who
knows the tale of the Patriarchs, as he knows
fairy stories or nursery rhymes, sees in the
morning of his own life a vision of the morning
of time. He has a standard by which he can
distinguish the enduring from the transient in
the life of man. He may never consciously
apply this standard. Yet it is likely to remain
in his mind and to influence his judgments.
The Bible, read in childhood, makes us love
those things which are best worth loving and
which have been tested by the experience of
ages. The fact that it came from the East
and has been naturalized in the West, that
the Englishman has fathered what the Jew so
long ago begot, is a proof of its universal value.
It has endured a severer struggle for life than
any other book, and in the course of it has more
completely rid itself of everything that is
trivial and accidental and unfitted to survive.
Living as it does in our language more vigor-
ously than even the greatest works of our own
writers, it gives us a living memory of the

central past of the world ; so that we, who came into history so late and out of a dark northern byway, can look back across the shining Mediterranean to the primeval Meso-potamia, as if it were the cradle of our own race from which we had wandered, carrying with us westward the stories that were to last for ever through all vicissitudes of times and place.